Simply Scrumptious
MICROWAVING

A collection of recipes from simple everyday to elegant gourmet dishes. All recipes have been tested by professional home economists.

Mary Ann Feuchter Robinson ❦ Rosemary Dunn Stancil ❦ Lorela Nichols Wilkins

Fawcett Columbine • New York

A Fawcett Columbine Book
Published by Ballantine Books
Copyright © 1982 by Simply Scrumptious, Inc.

All rights reserved under International and Pan-American Copyright
Conventions. Published in the United States by Ballantine Books, a division
of Random House, Inc., New York, and simultaneously in Canada by
Random House of Canada Limited, Toronto.

Library of Congress Catalog Card Number: 85-90892

ISBN: 0-449-90174-2

This edition published by arrangement with Simply Scrumptious, Incorporated
Illustrated by Kay Loftis Lambert
Editorial Consultant: Joe H. Wilkins, Jr.

Manufactured in the United States of America

First Ballantine Books Trade Edition: March 1986

10 9 8 7 6 5 4 3 2 1

Acknowledgements

Thanks to Joye H. Spates for her confidence and abiding faith in our abilities; and to Linda B. Wall for her inspiration and encouragement.

Thanks to our many friends for all their support.

Special Thanks to our Parents:

    Mr. & Mrs. John Charles Feuchter
    Mr. & Mrs. John T. Dunn
    Mr. & Mrs. Guy T. Nichols

Table of Contents

Introduction to
Simply Scrumptious Microwaving

The microwave oven is a unique cooking appliance that is becoming an indispensable piece of equipment in the kitchen. It is not intended to replace either the conventional range top or oven. However, with experience you may easily find yourself using it for 80% to 90% of your cooking. Results achieved with the microwave oven depend on the cook who operates the oven. Remember, you control the microwave oven and the food that is prepared. As with conventional cooking, do not be afraid to experiment and learn to use the microwave in your own style, utilizing your skills, talents and creativity.

For good results, it is necessary to learn recommended techniques for determining doneness of various foods and make judgements as the food cooks. Also, it is very important that you be familiar with the Owner's Manual that came with your microwave.

The authors of this book have converted numerous "old favorite" recipes to microwaving. Many recipes in this book provide a guide for food preparation with a back-to-basics approach, emphasizing the natural goodness and ease of "scratch" cooking in the microwave. For example, you will find many recipes using fresh vegetables and fruits, giving a straight-from-the-garden taste — with little seasoning necessary. All recipes used in SIMPLY SCRUMPTIOUS MICROWAVING have been tested and developed for accuracy by professional home economists, making this a book that will please and delight you for years to come.

TIMING ADJUSTMENTS: All recipes that appear in SIMPLY SCRUMPTIOUS MICROWAVING have been developed and tested using 600 to 700 watt microwave units. Know what your oven's wattage is and make adjustments accordingly, using this chart.

   400 to 500 watt unit: Add 30 seconds to each minute of cooking time.
   500 to 600 watt unit: Add 15 seconds to each minute of cooking time.

Cook the shortest amount of time that is recommended and add more time if necessary. After preparing recipes in this book you may find it convenient to note the times and power settings which work best in your oven.

POWER SETTING: Recipes in this book are designed to be used with all types of microwave ovens. The term HIGH means full or 100% power. Reduced power levels such as 80%, 70%, 50%, 30% or 10% are used because different manufacturers assign different names to levels of power. Check your owner's manual or oven cookbook to find settings on your oven that correspond to the percentage settings found in this book.

UTENSILS: Begin with what you have. Many "microwave utensils" are already in your kitchen even though you may have never considered using them for cooking.

GLASS: Most types of glass may be used for heating. For primary cooking, use only HEAT TEMPERED GLASS. Heat from the food will break glass that is not heat tempered. Glass measuring cups make excellent utensils.

PAPER: Paper products are an excellent choice for heating foods and as coverings to absorb moisture and splattering during cooking. Paper cups, plates, napkins, towels and wax paper are examples.

PLASTIC: Other than those designed especially for microwave use, plastic containers should be used for reheating only.

CHINA, STONEWARE, POTTERY AND PORCELAIN: Most dinnerware is suitable for heating foods. Some dinnerware, however, does contain materials that will absorb microwave energy and cause the dish to become hot and possibly break. If in doubt, test the dish. To test, measure 1/2 - 1 cup water in a cup. Place the cup of water and dish in the oven. Water cup can be placed in or on the dish. Microwave on HIGH 1-2 minutes. If the dish remains cool, it is suitable for microwaving. If the dish feels hot, it is not suitable for microwaving because it could become too hot during cooking and break. Never use a dish with metal trim, for example, a gold trim. The metalic trim may discolor and dish could break.

WOOD, STRAW AND SEASHELLS: Wood and other natural materials are suitable if the cooking time is very short. For example, warming a basket of dinner rolls for 1 minute. Wood has a tendency to absorb moisture and fats which cause it to heat up, dry out, and ultimately split if exposed to long periods of cooking.

METAL: Metal should not be used as a primary cooking utensil because microwaves can not pass through metal. Some microwave ovens allow limited use of metal. Examples are aluminum foil for shielding, frozen convenience dinner trays with sides that measure less than 3/4 inch and metal skewers filled with food. (Be sure to check your oven manufacturers use and care manual.)

DISH SHAPE. Foods cook more evenly in round dishes than square or rectangular-shaped ones. If you cook in square-shaped dishes, shielding the corners is often advised to prevent overcooking. Donut shaped dishes are excellent for foods that do not need to be stirred during microwaving, because energy penetrates food from the center, sides, top and bottom for more even cooking.

ARRANGEMENT: It is important to minimize differences in shape and density of food in order to assure uniform cooking. Place less dense or thinner areas toward the center of the dish, with more dense and thicker areas to the outside. Examples might be:

When cooking several potatoes, place smaller ones to the center,

When cooking chicken legs, place meaty parts to outside of the dish.

Place broccoli flowerets in the center with tougher stems to the outside. Rearrange foods that can't be stirred midway through cooking time to help foods cook more evenly.

FACTORS DETERMINING COOKING TIME:

STARTING TEMPERATURE: It is necessary to make timing adjustments when using refrigerated or very warm ingredients. If a cold food is put in the microwave oven, the cooking time will be longer.

VOLUME: The larger the volume of food to be microwaved, the longer the cooking time. When doubling a recipe, increase the time by about 1/2 and check for doneness, adding time if necessary.

DENSITY: Dense, heavy foods take longer to microwave than porous, airy ones. Food will also change in density, depending on the way it is prepared. Beef roast is denser than ground beef; mashed potatoes will not hold heat as long as a baked potato. Foods that have a high level of sugar or fat also cook quickly.

STIRRING: Cooking time is shortened by stirring and rearranging, equalizing the internal temperature by bringing the hotter outside areas to the cooler center portion.

COVERING: In microwaving, covering serves the same purpose as in conventional cooking. The cover holds in steam to tenderize food, keep it moist and shorten cooking time. A general rule is—If you would cover conventionally, cover during microwaving. When tight covers are needed such as when cooking rice, use plastic wrap. Loose coverings like paper towels or wax paper prevent splattering.

MOISTURE, FAT AND SUGAR: Cooking time is affected by the amount of moisture, fat and sugar present in the food being microwaved. Foods containing high fat and sugar levels heat very quickly and may reach higher temperatures than foods having low fat and sugar levels. Foods having lower fat and sugar levels require longer cooking time.

LINE VOLTAGE: Differences in line voltage to your home may cause difference in cooking time. For example, a cup of coffee may take 1 1/2 minutes to heat one day and 2 minutes to heat the next day. This may occur because the line voltage can vary from day to day, season to season and time of day. If you live in a rural area, your oven may cook faster than the same model in a large city. If you live at the end of a cul-de-sac your oven may cook slower. Voltage fluctuates and is lower during periods of peak consumption. An oven may cook slower on extremely hot or cold days when more electricity is being used. Line voltage fluctuations affect other appliances too, but because of the speed at which the microwave oven cooks food, these fluctuations are more noticeable. Often seconds of cooking time make a difference in the quality of the finished product. Some ovens are engineered with an automatic voltage regulator to sense fluctuations in line voltage. The oven automatically adds cooking time to compensate for fluctuations.

EXTENSION CORDS: The microwave oven should never be set up to operate on an extension cord.

ROTATING: If your oven has an even cooking pattern, this procedure is not necessary. Follow your manufacturer's directions.

SHIELDING: The purpose of shielding is to slow down the cooking process, preventing less dense areas from overcooking. Use small pieces of foil (if permitted in your oven) to shield areas that may overcook. For example, shielding is usually necessary on chicken wings and drumsticks and large pieces of meat, where some sections may cook faster than desired.

STANDING TIME: To prevent overcooking, it is very important that you allow for standing time. Foods continue to cook by internal heat when removed from the oven. The cooking process will continue for 1-15 minutes depending on the size, shape and density of the food being cooked.

CONVERTING RECIPES: To convert a recipe for use in the microwave, find a similar microwave recipe and start with the same amount of the main ingredients. Reduce liquids by 1/4 and use slightly less seasonings. Reduce conventional time by 1/4 to 1/3.

Simply Scrumptious
Appetizers & Beverages

Appetizers & Beverages

Appetizers

Beverages

General Guidelines

It is possible for the hostess to join the party and relax by using the microwave! Follow the suggestions listed below for successful appetizers and beverages:

Remember that many appetizers have heat sensitive ingredients such as cheese, sour cream, mayonnaise, eggs or meats that need to be cooked on a lower power setting. A setting between 50 to 70% power is usually recommended.

Select crackers for appetizers that are sturdy since the microwave does not dry food. Prepare appetizer fillings before the party, but do not place on crackers until just before ready to microwave or the base will become soggy.

Remember, it is possible to heat many appetizers in serving pieces in the microwave.

Cover appetizers only when a recipe specifies.

Take advantage of the convenience of heating many beverages on HIGH until just before the boiling point is reached for full flavor.

Shrimp Appetizer Tree

A beautiful party decoration at Christmas time!
Decorate tree with an assortment of raw vegetables
along with the shrimp to look very festive!

General directions for cooking shrimp:

Arrange shrimp in baking dish in a single layer and cook on HIGH power 3-5
minutes per pound. Microwave for 1/2 the time and stir, bringing the shrimp
on the outside to the center. Microwave remaining time and when shrimp
turn pink and opaque, remove from oven and let stand covered 1-2 minutes.

Direction for making tree:

Select a styrofoam cone and cover completely with parsley, endive, or
mustard greens. Anchor greens on tree with floral wire picks and secure to
tray by using floral sticky tape. Secure shrimp and vegetables to tree with
colored party picks.

Toasted Pecans or Peanuts

Place 1 1/2 cups pecans or peanuts in a 9-inch pie plate and microwave on
HIGH for 5-6 minutes. Stir every 2 minutes. Add butter and salt at end of
cooking time if desired. (Peanuts may take slightly longer to roast).

Shrimply Scrumptious Spread
Quick and delicious served with crackers.

Yield 3 cups

1/2 pound defrosted salad shrimp
1 can (10 3/4-ounces) cream of shrimp soup
1 package (8-ounces) cream cheese
2 tablespoons chopped parsley or chives
1 teaspoon garlic salt
1 teaspoon horseradish
1 tablespoon lemon juice
2 tablespoons catsup

Place shrimp in a baking dish in a single layer and cover with plastic wrap. Microwave on HIGH 1 1/2 - 2 1/2 minutes, stirring after cooking 1 minute. Cook until shrimp turns pink and opaque. Set aside. Soften cream cheese for 45 seconds to 1 minute on 70% power and combine with cream of shrimp soup. Beat in electric mixer or food processor until smooth. Add shrimp, parsley, garlic salt, horseradish, lemon juice and catsup. Stir until mixed.

Scrumptious Crab Dip
Quick & Elegant.

Yield 3 cups

3/4 pound blue crab meat, fresh or pasteurized
12 ounces sharp Cheddar cheese, grated
8 ounces Monterey Jack cheese, grated
1/3 cup half-and-half
1/2 cup dry white wine
1/2 teaspoon white pepper
2 garlic cloves, minced

Place milk in a 2-quart casserole. Microwave on 50% power 2-3 minutes until hot, but not boiling. Add cheeses and garlic, stirring to blend. Microwave for 4-6 minutes at 50%, stirring vigorously every 2 minutes with a wire whip or fork. Add crab meat, wine and pepper and cook 2 additional minutes. Transfer to a chafing dish set on low heat. Serve with toasted bread cubes or sesame sticks.

Spicy Pups

1 jar (10 ounce) currant jelly
4 tablespoons prepared mustard
1 pound frankfurters

Place jelly and mustard in 1 1/2-quart glass casserole. Beat well with wire whisk or rotary beater as mustard is added and microwave on 70% power 3-5 minutes. Cut franks crosswise into bite size pieces. Add to jelly and mustard mixture and cook for 3-5 minutes on HIGH until franks are hot. Place in chafing dish and use picks to serve with.

Basic Cream Cheese Spread

1 (8 ounce) package cream cheese
Grated onion
1/4 teaspoon salt
1/4 teaspoon white pepper

Soften cream cheese in microwave 1 - 1 1/2 minutes on 70% power. Add onion, salt and white pepper along with your favorite variation listed below.

Cucumber sandwiches. Grate 1/2 cup cucumber and add cream cheese mixture, stirring to blend.

Shrimp spread. Add 1 cup deveined shrimp to cream cheese mixture adding sour cream or milk until right consistency is reached.

Cream cheese and pimento spread. Add pimento and 2 teaspoons dry sherry, stirring to blend.

Green onion and cream cheese. Add 1/2 cup finely chopped green onion instead of grated onion to basic cream cheese spread.

Pineapple spread. Add pineapple preserves and ground nuts to an 8-ounce package of cream cheese and stir to blend.

Party Sandwiches

1 (8 ounce) package of cream cheese
1/4 cup finely chopped bell pepper
1/4 cup grated onion
3 tablespoons pimento
3 hard cooked eggs, finely chopped
1 cup finely chopped pecans
1 teaspoon salt
1/2 teaspoon white pepper

Soften cream cheese for 2 minutes on 50% power. Stir in remaining ingredients and microwave for 2-3 additional minutes to blend flavors.

Sandwich Fan

Make an interesting sandwich display by cutting a paper pattern in a fan shape. Cut bread shapes from the pattern and use varying colors and fillings on each row. Garnish with cheese, chives, olives and leeks, etc.

Sweet and Celery Nuts

2 tablespoons butter
1 cup peanuts
1 cup pecan halves
1 teaspoon celery salt
1 cup raisins

Microwave butter for 30-40 seconds. Add nuts and celery salt, stirring until nuts are coated with butter. Cook on HIGH for 6 minutes, stirring every two minutes. Add raisins. Serve warm.

Saucy Crab Ball

Makes a nice showing with crab mounded on top.

1 pound crab meat
1 pound cream cheese, softened
1 small onion, diced fine
1 teaspoon lemon juice
1/4 jar Crosse & Blackwell Cocktail sauce
Garlic powder to taste
Worcestershire sauce to taste

Microwave cream cheese for 1-2 minutes on 50% power. Add everything except crab meat and cocktail sauce. Form a ball. Mound crab over top of ball and top with cocktail sauce. Serve with bite size pastry shells, toast points or bland crackers.

Braunschweiger

1 pound braunschweiger (liverwurst)
1/2 teaspoon garlic powder
1/2 teaspoon basil
1/4 cup minced onions

Coating:

8 ounce package cream cheese
1/8 - 1/4 teaspoon Tabasco
1 teaspoon mayonnaise
Garlic powder to taste

Soften braunschweiger for 20 seconds on HIGH and then add garlic powder, basil and onions. Shape into ball or mound. To make coating, soften cream cheese 45 seconds to 1 minute on HIGH. Add Tabasco, mayonnaise and add garlic powder to taste. Ice the braunschweiger with the cream cheese mixture. Garnish and serve with crackers.

Garnish with black olives, dill or parsley sprigs.
Use canapé cutters to cut sliced cheese into desired shapes.

Use a microwave-safe corn popper for cooking rice or steaming a whole head of cauliflower.

Quick Pizza Fondue
Children love this dish!

6 servings

1 (10 ounce) can condensed Cheddar cheese soup
2 tablespoons catsup
1/2 teaspoon oregano
Dash of garlic powder or a diced garlic clove
1 cup cheese (Swiss or sharp Cheddar)

Microwave soup for 3-4 minutes on 70% power. Stir and add remaining ingredients. Microwave for 1-2 minutes on 50% power. Serve with bite size pieces of French bread, apples, celery or green peppers.

Beef Dip
Quick, easy and spicy!

Yield: 2 cups

1 (8-ounce) package cream cheese
1 (2 1/2 ounce) package dried beef (chopped fine)
2 tablespoons diced onion
2 tablespoons milk
1/4 cup sour cream
3/4 teaspoon black pepper

Soften cheese in microwave for 1-2 minutes on 70% power. Mix other ingredients together with cheese and microwave 3-4 minutes on 70% power stirring halfway through cooking time.

Artichoke Pan Quiche
Scrumptious as a hot appetizer!

Yield 6-8 servings per Quiche

1/3 cup onion, chopped
1 garlic clove, minced
4 eggs
1 (14 ounce) can artichoke hearts, drained and chopped
   (2 cups of grated zucchini may be substituted)
1/4 cup bread crumbs
1/2 pound Swiss cheese, grated
2 tablespoons chopped parsley
1/2 teaspoon each of oregano, salt and Tabasco

Microwave onions and garlic clove for 1-2 minutes on HIGH. Beat eggs and add remaining ingredients. Place mixture in two 8-inch square dishes. (Freeze one for later if desired). Shield corners with foil if oven permits use of metal. Microwave 10-12 minutes at 70% power. Let stand 5 minutes before serving.

Ham Cheese Rolls

Do ahead and freeze.
Great to serve at a buffet or luncheon.

60 servings

1 pound grated ham
1 cup butter at room temperature
3 tablespoons poppy seed
1 teaspoon Worcestershire sauce
3 tablespoons mustard
1 medium onion, grated
3/4 pound Swiss cheese, grated
3 packages party rolls (such as Peppridge Farm)

Mix all ingredients except rolls. Slice rolls and fill with mixture. To serve, place rolls on towel-lined plate in a circle. To heat 12 rolls, microwave on 70% power 1 - 1 1/2 minutes.

Shrimp Mold

A tasty appetizer that is very attractive on a buffet table.

1 pound small shrimp, microwaved and cut up
8 ounce cream cheese
1 can shrimp soup (frozen is best)
2 tablespoons catsup
3/4 cup mayonnaise
1/2 cup green pepper, diced
1/2 cup celery, diced
1/4 cup onion, grated
1 envelope unflavored gelatin (Use 1 1/2 envelopes unflavored gelatin
    if mold won't be eaten quickly)

Cover and cook shrimp for 3 - 4 1/2 minutes until they turn pink and opaque and set aside. Microwave soup for 1-2 minutes on HIGH. Soften cream cheese on 70% power 45 seconds. Soften gelatin in 2 tablespoons of cold water and add cream cheese and soup. Stir well, adding remaining ingredients. Pour in fish mold and chill until serving time.

Decorations for making Fish Mold:

It is necessary to make a clear gelatin glaze first to pour in fish mold so raw vegetables will stay in place.

1. Garnish inside of mold by using radish slices for fish scales, olive slices for eyes, strips of carrots, green pepper or thinly sliced celery for fins.

2. Soften 1 package unflavored gelatin in 1/4 cup water. Add 1 cup water and microwave on HIGH 1-2 minutes to dissolve gelatin. Gently spoon a little gelatin mixture into mold. Refrigerate to set. Slowly build up gelatin in mold until all is used. Then pour shrimp mixture over glaze and refrigerate until set.

Sugared Pecans

1 1/2 cups pecan halves
1 tablespoon butter
1/4 cup sugar
1/2 teaspoon cinnamon

Melt butter in a 9-inch pie plate. Stir in pecan halves, sugar and cinnamon and cook for 2 minutes on HIGH. Stir and cook for 2 more minutes. Reduce power to 70% and microwave 1 - 1 1/2 additional minutes.

Herbed Cream Cheese Mold
Prepare a week before the party to blend flavors.
Refrigerate.

8 ounces cream cheese
1/3 cup sour cream
3 tablespoons green onion, chopped
1/2 cup parsley
1 teaspoon garlic salt
1/4 teaspoon freshly ground pepper
1 teaspoon dried tarragon
1 teaspoon chives

Soften cheese for 1 1/2 to 2 minutes at 50% power. Add remaining ingredients and mix well. Pour into mold and chill. Serve with crackers or Melba toast.
Garnish as desired.

Low-Cal Stuffed Mushrooms

8 ounces large mushrooms
3 medium green onions
2 teaspoons sour cream
1 teaspoon lemon juice
1/2 teaspoon seasoned garlic salt

Remove stems from mushrooms and finely chop. Thinly slice green onions including tops. Mix with mushroom stems. Microwave on HIGH for 2-3 minutes. Add sour cream, lemon juice and garlic salt. Fill mushroom caps and place 10-12 filled caps on pie pan. Microwave for 2-3 minutes on 80% power.

Artichoke Dip
So easy to prepare and so delicious!

Yields 3 cups dip

1 (14 ounce) can artichoke hearts
1 cup mayonnaise
1 cup grated Parmesan cheese
1 tablespoon lemon juice, optional
2 garlic cloves, minced
1/2 teaspoon pepper, white preferred
1/4 teaspoon salt

Drain artichokes well, squeezing out all juice. Chop into small pieces. Add remaining ingredients and place in 8-inch square casserole. Cook on HIGH 2 minutes. Stir and cook 5-7 minutes at 50% power. Allow to stand 5 minutes before serving. Then serve hot with Melba toast rounds or other crackers.

Crab Stuffed Mushrooms

1 pound large mushrooms
3 tablespoons butter
1 tablespoon flour
1/2 cup milk
Salt and white pepper to taste
1/2 cup green onion, finely chopped
1 (6-ounce) package frozen crabmeat, thawed
1 tablespoon dry sherry or white wine
1 egg yolk
1/3 cup Parmesan cheese

Remove mushroom stems and set aside. Microwave mushroom caps, hollow-side down in baking dish for 3-5 minutes on HIGH. Drain, add 1 tablespoon butter and toss.

Make white sauce. Melt 1 tablespoon butter, add 1 tablespoon flour and stir to blend. Add 1/2 cup milk and cook on 70% power for 1 minute, stirring once. Add salt, pepper, sherry or wine and Parmesan cheese. Stir and add crabmeat. Set aside.

Microwave green onions for 1 minute on HIGH. Add to crabmeat mixture. Stuff mushroom caps and sprinkle with additional Parmesan cheese if desired. Microwave 8-10 minutes on 70% power, or until hot. Serve at once.

To make the best lemonade, prepare syrup the day before serving. In a 1-quart container dissolve 1 1/2 cups sugar and 1 tablespoon finely grated lemon peel with 1 1/2 cups water in the microwave for 3-4 minutes on HIGH power. Add 1 1/2 cups lemon juice and refrigerate until serving time. To make lemonade, mix 1/4 cup syrup with 3/4 cup cold water (or club soda). Yield 16 1-cup servings.

Pecan Worcestershire
Delicious with a Bloody Mary!

Yield: 1 1/2 cup nuts

1 tablespoon butter
2 tablespoons Lea and
 Perrins Worcestershire Sauce
1 dash of hot sauce
Salt and pepper to taste
1 1/2 cups pecan halves

Melt butter in a 9-inch pie plate. Add Worcestershire sauce, hot sauce and pecan halves, stirring to coat nuts. Cook for 5-6 minutes on HIGH, stirring every two minutes, making sure nuts from outside are moved to the center. Salt and pepper to taste and allow to stand 5-10 minutes before serving.

Cheese-Sour Cream Fondue

6 slices bacon
1/4 cup minced onion
2 teaspoons all-purpose flour
1 teaspoon Worcestershire sauce
1 pound sharp Cheddar cheese, grated
2 cups sour cream

Microwave bacon 6-8 minutes at 100% power. Reserve one tablespoon of bacon drippings and sauté onions 45 seconds on HIGH. Stir in flour and add remaining ingredients. Microwave at 50% power for 9-12 minutes until cheese melts. Pour into fondue pot. Top with bacon and place over fondue burner.

"Do Your Own Thing Dip"
Use fresh vegetables as dippers for this tasty appetizer!

1 (8-ounce) package cream cheese
1/2 cup sour cream or salad dressing
2-3 chopped green onions
1/2 teaspoon white pepper

Microwave cream cheese in glass mixing bowl about 2 minutes on 70% power. Add sour cream or salad dressing along with green onion and white pepper.

Variation:

Hot Vegetable Dip: Add 1 cup chopped fresh broccoli or spinach, one cup finely chopped fresh mushrooms, 5 slices crumbled bacon, ½ cup finely grated Parmesan cheese and 1 tablespoon fresh lemon juice. Mix well with above cream cheese mixture. Microwave for 2-3 minutes on 70% power until warm, allowing flavors to blend. Even children like this—because they don't know what they are eating!

Wrapped Chicken Livers

20 appetizers

1/2 cup medium dry sherry
1 1/2 teaspoons dry mustard
1/4 teaspoon hot pepper sauce
1/2 teaspoon salt
10 chicken livers (3/4 pound)
10 slices bacon, cut in half

Cut livers in half and marinate in a mixture of sherry, mustard, hot pepper sauce and salt. Cover with plastic wrap and let set for several hours in the refrigerator. Stir several times. Cook bacon for 3-4 minutes on HIGH. Drain liver and wrap bacon around each piece, securing with wooden tooth picks. Arrange 10 appetizers around edge of plate and cook on HIGH for 3-4 minutes. Repeat process with remaining appetizers.

Deviled Mushrooms

12 appetizers

12 medium mushrooms (1 1/2 inch)
1/2 cup minced ham
2 tablespoons chopped shallots
1/4 cup bell pepper
1 tablespoon prepared mustard
2 teaspoons mayonnaise
2 tablespoons butter
Dash of pepper
Green olives for garnish

Remove mushroom stems (not needed here, so save for use later) and place mushroom caps in a 9-inch glass dish. Cover and microwave 1-2 minutes on HIGH. Drain. Sprinkle with salt and add ham, shallots, bell pepper, mustard, butter and pepper. Mix and spoon into mushroom caps topping with green olive slices. Cook on HIGH for 2 1/2 - 3 minutes. Let stand 2 or 3 minutes. Place on platter, garnish and serve at once!

Cheese Stuffed Mushrooms

1 pound small fresh mushrooms
1/2 pound Swiss cheese, grated
1/2 cup bread crumbs
Parsley flakes
White wine
1/4 teaspoon white pepper

Remove mushroom stems and cut into small pieces. Sauté in 1 tablespoon butter. Add 1 teaspoon parsley flakes. Cook on HIGH for 2 minutes. Mix in cheese and bread crumbs. Add about 1 tablespoon wine to moisten. Stuff mushroom caps and place in circular position to cook. If preparing all mushrooms at one time, cook on HIGH for 8-10 minutes or until hot and cheese melts.

Apple Cheese Ball
A very tasty change of pace!

Yields 2 1/2 cups

12 ounces of cream cheese
1 apple, unpeeled
1/2 cup green onion, finely sliced
1/2 teaspoon salt
1/4 teaspoon white pepper
2 tablespoons apple juice
1 - 1 1/2 cups shredded Cheddar cheese
1/2 cup chopped walnuts
3 tablespoons fresh parsley, finely chopped

Microwave cream cheese in glass mixing bowl for 1 1/2 - 2 minutes on 70% power until softened. Core apple and chop into small pieces. Add chopped apple, onion, salt, pepper and apple juice to cream cheese. Microwave for 2-4 minutes on 50% power to blend flavors. Add Cheddar cheese and chill for easier shaping. Form into ball and roll in chopped parsley and nuts.

Mystery Cheese Ball

12 ounces cream cheese
8 ounces extra sharp Cracker Barrel cheese
1/4 pound bleu cheese
1 cup chopped parsley
1 cup chopped pecans or walnuts
1 garlic clove, minced
3 tablespoons Worcestershire sauce
1/4 teaspoon red pepper

Microwave cream cheese for 2 minutes on 50% power to soften slightly. Add 1/2 cup parsley and 1/2 cup nuts, along with remaining ingredients. Form into a ball, and then roll the ball in the remaining nuts and parsley.

Cheese Bites
A quick appetizer for unexpected guests!

8 servings

6-8 English muffins
1 cup chopped black olives
1 1/2 cups sharp Cheddar cheese
1/2 cup grated onion
1/2 teaspoon curry powder
1/4 teaspoon salt

Top English muffins with well mixed cheese mixture. Place muffins on a paper towel-lined container. Microwave for 3-4 minutes on 80% power until bubbly. Quarter and serve.

Spinach Dip
A delicious quickie for raw vegetables.

Yield 2 cups dip

1 (10-ounce) package chopped frozen spinach
2 tablespoons minced onion
1 cup mayonnaise
1/2 package Ranch Style dressing mix
1 teaspoon lemon juice

Defrost frozen spinach for 2 minutes on HIGH. Squeeze excess water out and add remaining ingredients.

Cream Cheese and
Dried Beef Appetizer

Cut in squares and serve as a quiche.

8 ounces cream cheese
2 tablespoons milk
2 eggs
2 1/2 ounces chopped dried beef
2 tablespoons onions, minced
1/4 cup chopped green pepper
1/2 teaspoon garlic powder
1/4 teaspoon black pepper (freshly ground is best)
1/2 cup sour cream
1/2 cup pecans or walnuts
2 tablespoons butter

Soften cream cheese for 2 minutes at 50% power. Sauté nuts in 2 table-spoons butter for 2 minutes on HIGH. Add remaining ingredients and mix well. Pour in 8-inch square baking dish and microwave for 8 minutes on 70% power.

When cooking popcorn in the microwave do so only in a popcorn pop-per designed for the microwave. (Otherwise there is danger of fire).

Spicy Meat Balls
Liquid Smoke is the secret ingredient in this recipe!

Yield 3 dozen appetizers

1 pound ground round beef
1/2 cup onion, finely chopped
2 tablespoons green pepper, finely chopped
1 egg, beaten
2 tablespoons milk
1/2 cup bread crumbs
1 teaspoon garlic salt
1/2 teaspoon black pepper

Sauce:

1 1/2 cups catsup
1/4 cup dark brown sugar, packed
1 tablespoon mustard
2 tablespoons vinegar
1 tablespoon Worcestershire sauce
2-3 teaspoons Liquid Smoke

In a large bowl combine beef, onion, green pepper, egg, milk, bread crumbs, garlic salt and pepper. Toss lightly until mixed. Form into about 3 dozen meat balls. Place in a baking dish in a single layer. Microwave uncovered on 70% power for 3-5 minutes. Stir to rearrange bringing the meatballs on the outside to the center. Cook on 70% power 2-3 additional minutes until just done. (Some meat balls may still be pink but will finish cooking upon standing). Drain and cover with foil.

While meat stands combine the sauce ingredients. Microwave sauce for 3-4 minutes on HIGH power. Add sauce to meatballs and cook on 70% power 3-5 minutes stirring once.

Swiss Cheese Fondue
A fun dish to serve for a crowd!

1 pound Swiss cheese, grated
2 cups dry white wine
Dash of nutmeg
2 tablespoons cornstarch
3 tablespoons Kirsch or 4 tablespoons cognac
2 garlic cloves
1/2 teaspoon salt and paprika

Rub cooking utensil with minced garlic. Pour in wine and microwave at HIGH power for 3-4 minutes, or just before boiling. Add cheese by the handful, stirring to mix well. Microwave on 70% power for 3-6 minutes until cheese melts. Dissolve cornstarch in Kirsch or cognac and add to fondue. Mix in nutmeg, salt and paprika. Serve with French bread.

🐟 Toast bread for hot sandwiches conventionally because bread will have more body and won't get soggy during heating.

Hot Mocha Mix

Serves 60

1 cup cocoa
1/2 cup instant coffee
2 cups powdered sugar
2 cups instant nonfat dry milk
2 cups nondairy creamer

Combine all ingredients and mix well. Store in air tight container.

To serve, heat 1 cup of water about 2 minutes. Place 2 tablespoons mix in cup and stir well.

Hot Cocoa

Yield 5 to 6 servings

4 cups milk
1 cup boiling water
4 tablespoons cocoa
1/2 cup sugar
1 teaspoon vanilla

Combine cocoa and sugar in 2-quart glass measure or simmer pot. Add water and mix to blend. Microwave on HIGH for 3 to 4 minutes. Stir occasionally until syrup boils.

Add milk and cook on HIGH until mixture is hot but not boiling. Stir in vanilla and beat with wire wisk. Serve at once.

French Hot Chocolate

Yield 10-12 cups

1 cup semi-sweet real chocolate pieces
1/2 cup light corn syrup
1/4 cup water
1 teaspoon vanilla
1 cup whipping cream
2 quarts milk

Place chocolate, corn syrup and water in a 1-quart measuring container. Microwave 2 - 2 1/2 minutes on HIGH, stirring several times until chips melt. Chill.

Whip cream until soft peaks form. Slowly add cooked chocolate and continue whipping until mixture holds its shape.

For one cup, heat 1/2 cup of milk until almost boiling. Fill cup with chocolate mixture and stir.

To make 10 to 12 servings heat 2 quarts of milk on HIGH 12 to 16 minutes. Proceed as above.

Spiced Tea

10 servings

6 whole cloves
1 quart water
1 cup orange juice
3 tablespoons lemon juice

1 stick cinnamon
3 teaspoons tea, heaping
1 cup pineapple juice
2/3 cup sugar

Place cinnamon and cloves in 2 cups of water and microwave on HIGH 5 minutes. Simmer at 50% power 5 additional minutes. Strain. Make tea in other two cups of water by heating until water boils. Let steep 5 minutes before straining. Add remaining ingredients and heat on HIGH for 14 to 16 minutes.

Cranberry Punch

serves 15

1 quart cranberry juice
1 quart unsweetened pineapple juice
2 cups water
1/3 cup brown sugar
1 1/2 teaspoon whole allspice
2 cinnamon sticks
1 lemon quartered

Tie spices in cheese cloth (or strain later) and place all ingredients in microwave proof dish. Microwave on HIGH 24 minutes and 50% power 10 additional minutes.

Hot Scotch
Kids love it!

1 mug of milk
2-3 tablespoons butterscotch chips

Heat a mug of milk 1-1 1/2 minutes on HIGH. Add chips and stir. Garnish with a marshmallow and enjoy!

Janie's Bloody Marys

2 quarts tomato juice
4 lemons, juiced
Tabasco sauce to taste
5 tablespoons Worcestershire sauce
2 beef bouillon cubes
4 teaspoons Lowry's seasoned salt
1 1/2 pint of Vodka (optional)

Heat bouillon in 2 cups of tomato juice until dissolved for 4 to 5 minutes. Mix with remaining ingredients. Good with or without vodka.

Hot Tomato Bouillon
Great on a cold day.

Yield 14 small cups

1 can tomato soup
1 can beef broth
1 (13 1/2-ounce) can tomato juice
1 (6-ounce) can V8 juice
1 teaspoon Lowry's seasoned salt
1/4 teaspoon thyme
1/2 teaspoon cream style horseradish
1 tablespoon Worcestershire sauce

Place all ingredients into large simmer pot and heat to blend flavors. Serve hot.

Special Cocoa Mix
"Makes a large batch to share with Chocolate lovers."

1 can (2 lb.) of chocolate drink mix
1 (1 lb.) jar of non-dairy creamer
1 (14-ounce) box powdered dry milk
1 cup powdered sugar

Mix in large bowl and store in air tight container. Prepare by the cup in the microwave by heating water about 2 minutes on HIGH and adding 3 heaping teaspoons of mix.

This mixture has very little sediment and dissolves easily.

Café Brulot

8 to 10 servings

1 4-inch cinnamon stick
12 whole cloves
Peel of one orange cut in one spiral piece
Peel of one lemon cut in one spiral piece
6 teaspoons sugar
6 ounces brandy
2 ounces Triple Sec
1 quart of strong black coffee

In large chafing dish liner or other container add cinnamon, cloves, orange and lemon peel, sugar and Triple Sec. Heat to simmer and carry to table. Add brandy; flame, and stir until sugar is dissolved. Gradually add hot black coffee and continue mixing until flame flickers. Serve hot in small cups.

Add marshmallows to cocoa during the last 15 seconds of heating. Children enjoy watching this process.

Instant Spiced Tea Mix

Serves 60

3/4 cup lemon flavored instant tea
1/2 to 3/4 cup sugar
2 cups powdered orange breakfast drink
2 teaspoons cinnamon
1/4 teaspoon cloves
1/2 teaspoon allspice

Mix ingredients together and store in tightly covered container.

For each serving, heat water about 2 minutes on HIGH and add 2 to 2 1/2 heaping teaspoons of mix for each cup of water.

Garnish with orange or lemon slice and whole clove.

Punch for a Bunch
Inexpensive and delicious!

2 ounces citric acid (from pharmacy)
   powdered or liquid
1 quart boiling water
6 or 7 cups sugar
5 quarts cold water
1 (46-ounce) can pineapple juice
2 or 3 quarts of Ginger Ale

Microwave 1 quart of water to boiling point. Add citric acid and sugar. Stir to dissolve and let stand overnight in plastic or glass container. Add remaining ingredients and mix using food coloring to get desired color.

Serves 50 to 60.

When stirring instant cocoa, tea, or coffee into water boiled in the microwave, put a small amount of mix in first and stir, thus preventing foaming over the top of the cup.

Mulled Cider

10 servings

4 cups brewed tea
4 cups apple cider
1/2 cup brown sugar
1 cinnamon stick
1 teaspoon whole allspice
1 teaspoon whole cloves

Microwave sugar and two cups of cider about 5 minutes on HIGH to dissolve sugar. Add remaining ingredients. Microwave on HIGH 16 to 18 minutes. Strain spices. Pour into cider bowl and garnish with baked apples.

Cut peeling from 4 apples in flower design and microwave on HIGH 4 to minutes. Stud apples with cloves and float apples in mulled cider bowl.

Hot Buttered Rum
A great warmer upper for a cold day!

3/4 cup apple juice per mug
1 jigger dark rum
1 teaspoon butter
Dash of cinnamon per mug

Place apple juice in mug and heat to boiling. Add rum, butter and cinnamon. Garnish with thinly sliced lemon and cinnamon stick.

Christmas Wassail
Colonial Williamsburg Style

20 servings

1 cup sugar
1 lemon sliced thinly
2 cups orange juice
1/2 cup lemon juice

4 sticks cinnamon
2 cups pineapple juice
6 cups red wine of choice
1 cup dry sherry

Microwave sugar, cinnamon sticks and lemon slices in 1/2 cup water for 1 minute on HIGH and 4-5 minutes at 50% power. Strain and add to remaining ingredients.

Store until guests arrive and heat in cup as needed garnishing with lemon or orange slices. Microwave one cup on HIGH 1 1/2 - 2 minutes.

Save left-over coffee and microwave cup-by-cup as needed. There will be no bitter after-taste.

Simply Scrumptious
Soups, Salads, & Sandwiches

Soups, Salads & Sandwiches

Soups

Salads

Salad Dressings

Sandwiches

Soups - General Guidelines

Conventional soups must be cooked over low heat and stirred often to prevent sticking, but most can be microwaved on HIGH to the boiling point or serving temperature - 160°F. The temperature probe is helpful to prevent over-heating, especially with cream soups. Another big plus is that the utensil is easy to clean!

Mushrooms, clams, or other sensitive ingredients may need to cook at 70% POWER, or lower, to prevent popping.

Generally you should: cook soups covered, sauté vegetables to tenderize before adding to soup, and trim fat from meat so that the soup is not too greasy.

Microwave soups in a container with twice the volume of the ingredients so the mixture does not boil over. Milk "boils higher" in the microwave than conventionally.

Cream soups sometimes need more thickening than the conventional recipe because there is less moisture evaporation during cooking.

Soup mix containing dehydrated rice or noodles needs to be cooked on a lower setting of 50% to allow the starch to rehydrate and soften.

Stock recipes and soups that require long, slow cooking to blend flavors or tenderize meat are offered in the Clay Pot Cookery chapter of *Simply Scrumptious*.

Salmon Chowder

1 large can salmon (bone and skin removed)
1 large baking potato
1 large onion, thinly sliced
1/4 cup butter
1 quart milk (may use half-and-half)
Salt and pepper to taste

Microwave potato 4-6 minutes on HIGH. Sauté onion in butter 1-2 minutes on HIGH. Peel and dice potatoes. Add all ingredients to onion and heat on HIGH to serving temperature.

OYSTER STEW. Substitute one 10-ounce can oysters (undrained) for salmon and add a dash of celery salt.

Homemade Vegetable Soup

2 cups fresh corn
1 cup fresh okra, sliced thin
2 cups cabbage, thinly sliced
1 cup carrots, thinly sliced
32-ounce can tomato juice, or plain tomatoes
2-3 cups chicken stock (homemade preferred)
1/4 cup bacon drippings
1 tablespoon sugar
1 teaspoon pepper
1 teaspoon basil
2 teaspoons salt

Place all fresh vegetables in large container and cover tightly (may use plastic wrap). Microwave 8-12 minutes on HIGH until done. Stir once or twice. Add remaining ingredients and cook on HIGH 15 minutes. Stir and cook covered 25-30 minutes on 50% POWER. Taste and adjust seasonings.

She-Crab Soup

1 medium onion, chopped
1 pound white crab meat
2 1/2 quarts milk
1 stick butter
Salt, pepper and Worcestershire to taste
1 teaspoon cornstarch
1/4 pound crab roe, chopped
1/2 cup sherry wine

Sauté onion and butter on HIGH 1-3 minutes. Add crab meat, milk with cornstarch dissolved in it and seasonings. Cook on HIGH just to boiling. Add crab roe and sherry. Stir together well. Sprinkle a little paprika on each serving and serve piping hot.

Tomato Bisque

serves 4-6

1 large can tomatoes (use fresh ones when in season)
2 cups half-and-half
1 teaspoon chicken bouillon granules
1/2 teaspoon basil*
1/4 teaspoon onion powder
Pinch of soda

Put tomatoes, including liquid, in blender and blend a few seconds to chop desired amount. Add all ingredients and microwave on HIGH to serving temperature, about 5 minutes.

*You may substitute sage for basil, if you prefer.

Southern Corn Chowder

1/2 cup chopped salt pork (may substitute 4 slices bacon)
1/2 cup sliced celery
1/2 cup green pepper, diced
1 medium onion, chopped
2 potatoes, microwaved and diced
1 bay leaf
1 teaspoon salt
1/4 cup flour
2 cups milk
1/2 cup light cream
2-3 cups fresh corn, cut from cob

Microwave salt pork 2-3 minutes on HIGH. Add onion, celery and pepper. Microwave 2-3 minutes. Mix flour with small amount of the milk and add to above mixture along with the diced potatoes. Add remaining milk, salt and bay leaf, and heat on HIGH until thickened. Add cream and corn. Microwave again on HIGH 4-6 minutes.

French Onion Soup

serves 4

4 large onions, thinly sliced
1/4 cup butter
1 (10 3/4-ounce) can beef broth
2-3 cups home made chicken stock,
    if possible (It is well worth the time
    and effort. See page 122 for recipe.)
1 (10 3/4-ounce) can chicken broth
1/4 cup sherry or white wine
1/2 teaspoon white or black pepper (white preferred)
2 slices boiled ham, sliced in thin strips (optional)
12 ounces Swiss cheese
1/2 cup Parmesan cheese

Combine onion and butter in 3-quart casserole. Cover with plastic wrap and microwave on HIGH for 6-10 minutes, until onions are semi-soft and translucent. Pour stock and broth over onions. Add ham and microwave 5-7 minutes until heated. Add sherry or wine. Ladle into 4 individual casseroles. Sprinkle with cheeses and microwave 6-8 minutes on HIGH. Serve with toasted French bread.

When converting a conventional soup recipe to microwave, reduce the amount of liquid, unless cooking dried beans or peas. Also reduce the salt and other seasonings.

Chicken and Artichoke Soup

Good appetizer soup.

serves 6

3 shallots
2 cloves garlic
1/2 stick butter
6 tablespoons flour
2 cups chicken stock
1 can artichoke hearts with liquid
2 teaspoons parsley flakes
1 bay leaf
1/4 teaspoon thyme
1 cup half-and-half
3/4 cup chicken, cooked and finely chopped

Sauté shallots, garlic and butter on HIGH 2 minutes. Add flour to make a roux. Add stock and half-and-half. Cook on HIGH about 1 1/2 minutes, until thickened. Stir and continue cooking on HIGH 2-4 minutes, just to boiling. Add spices, artichoke hearts and chicken. Heat to serving temperature.

 For added interest, cut croutons in shapes.

Quick Potato Soup

2 cups sliced, peeled potatoes (raw)
1/2 cup finely chopped leeks or onions
1 cup water
1 1/2 cups half-and-half
1 tablespoon butter
1/2 teaspoon salt
1/8 teaspoon pepper
4 thin slices favorite cheese (optional)
Bacon or chives for garnish

Microwave potatoes, onion and water on HIGH 8-10 minutes until potatoes are tender. Cover and let rest 5 minutes. Mash potatoes with a fork. Add remaining ingredients except cheese and cook on HIGH 5-8 minutes to serving temperature. Garnish with cheese and bacon, or chives.

VICHYSSOISE. Blend "Quick Potato Soup" in blender till smooth and chill. Serve garnished generously with chives.

CHOWDER. A variety of delicious chowders may be made by adding 1 cup of chicken or the vegetable of your choice to "Quick Potato Soup".

CLAM CHOWDER. Add 1 (7-ounce) can clams with liquid and 1/2 teaspoon celery salt to "Quick Potato Soup".

 Cutting meats and vegetables in small pieces of uniform size will help the soup cook more evenly.

Soup Supreme
Has a delicate flavor!

1/4 cup butter
1 small carrot, peeled and finely chopped
1 small stalk celery, finely chopped
1/2 onion, sliced in thin rings
1/2 cup finely grated Cheddar cheese (medium or sharp)
1/4 cup flour
2 cups chicken stock (If stock is not available, use 2 cups water and
    3 teaspoons chicken bouillon)
2 cups milk (or half-and-half)
1/3 cup finely chopped ham (optional)
Dash soda
Salt and white pepper

Cook butter, carrot, celery and onion covered on HIGH about 1 1/2 - 2 1/2 minutes, until vegetables are tender. Stir in flour; add milk, stock and dash of soda. Cook on HIGH 5-8 minutes until soup just starts to boil. Season to taste and add cheese and ham. Stir until cheese melts. Return to microwave and cook on HIGH about 1 minute or to serving temperature. Garnish with chives.

Soup Supreme
Cream Soup Variations

The best cream soups you've ever tasted may be made by using Soup Supreme as a base and adding the desired vegetable. We prefer to have pieces of vegetables in the soup for texture and interest, but if you prefer, purée the soup in the blender till it is the texture you like. Soup Supreme or cream soups make a tasty sauce or gravy over vegetables, meat, poultry, rice or pasta, too.

CREAM OF CAULIFLOWER SOUP. Add 1 small head cauliflower cut in small flowerets. Place in a covered dish with 1/4 cup water and microwave on HIGH 5-10 minutes. Drain well and add to "Soup Supreme".

CREAM OF BROCCOLI SOUP. Microwave two 10-ounce packages frozen broccoli on HIGH 8-10 minutes. Drain well and stir into "Soup Supreme". Garnish with croutons.

CREAM OF SPINACH SOUP. Add two 10-ounce packages frozen, chopped spinach. Microwave frozen spinach on HIGH 8-10 minutes. Drain well and stir into "Soup Supreme". Add a dash of tarragon or nutmeg, if desired. Garnish with fried bacon curls, chopped egg, or croutons.

CREAM OF CARROT SOUP. Add 1 cup sliced carrots (make a few carrot curls for garnish), 1 cup cooked rice, 1 teaspoon parsley flakes, dash of celery salt and cayenne. Place carrots in covered dish with 2 tablespoons water and microwave on HIGH 2-5 minutes. Drain and add with all other ingredients to "Soup Supreme".

CREAM OF ASPARAGUS SOUP. Microwave one 10-ounce package frozen asparagus pieces on HIGH 3-5 minutes and add to "Soup Supreme".

CREAM OF ARTICHOKE SOUP. Add 1 can drained chopped artichoke hearts to "Soup Supreme".

Egg Flower Soup

serves 4-6

1/2 pound lean pork, cut in fine strips
1 scallion or 1/2 onion
2 eggs, beaten
6 cups chicken broth
1 tablespoon cornstarch and 1/4 cup water
2 tablespoons soy sauce
1 teaspoon sherry
Dash pepper

Sauté onion and pork covered on HIGH 3-5 minutes. Add broth, soy, sherry, and pepper. Heat to boiling by cooking on HIGH 6-8 minutes. Slowly dribble beaten egg into boiling soup to form "flowers". Add cornstarch and water mixture and stir to thicken. Microwave a few minutes longer if needed.

Potato Sausage Soup
A quick hearty Supper Soup.

Yield - 5 cups

1/2 pound sausage
1 cup chopped onion
1/2 cup chopped celery
1 cup hot water
1/2 teaspoon rosemary, crushed
1/8 teaspoon garlic powder
1 teaspoon salt
1/8 teaspoon pepper
3/4 pound straight cut French Fries
    (or make your own from fresh potatoes)
1 1/2 cups milk
Parsley

Cook sausage, onion and celery on HIGH 4-6 minutes. Drain fat and add water, seasonings and potatoes. Cover and cook on HIGH 10 minutes, until potatoes are tender. Stir in milk and heat to serving temperature. Garnish with parsley.

Frozen bread can be quickly defrosted in the microwave. Approximately 1 minute on 80% power is sufficient for 2 slices of bread. Bread should be wrapped in paper towels or a cloth towel to absorb moisture.

Microwave soups usually need a little more thickening than conventional recipes.

Heat single servings of your favorite canned or dehydrated soups in minutes. Microwave on HIGH about 2 minutes per cup. Covering is not necessary but speeds heating time a little.

Dense purées, cream soups, seafood chowders and soups containing less tender cuts of meat should be cooked on a reduced power level.

Salads - General Guidelines

The microwave oven is very handy when making salads. Cooked vegetables will have a prettier color than ever. The flavor of meat salads will be better. Salad dressings are quick and easy.

The time factor in making salads is one big advantage. Water can be boiled quickly and cream cheese softened in a wink. Meats can be cooked in a breeze, and vegetables steamed in a hurry.

Apricot Salad
Good with anything and anytime!

1 (17 ounce) can apricots, drained and quartered (reserve juice)
1 (4 ounce) bottle maraschino cherries, halved (reserve juice)
1/4 cup cider vinegar
3 sticks cinnamon
1 tablespoon whole cloves
1 (3 ounce) package lemon gelatin
1 cup nuts, chopped

In a 4 cup measuring cup add enough water with apricot and cherry juice and vinegar to make 2 cups liquid. Add spices. Microwave on HIGH 3 minutes and then turn to 50% power for 7 minutes. Cover and let sit several minutes. Strain liquid. Add gelatin and stir until dissolved. Add fruit and nuts. Pour into mold. Chill.

Date Soufflé Salad
A good frozen salad!

serves 6 to 8

1 (8 ounce) package cream cheese
1/4 cup maple syrup
1 tablespoon lemon juice
1/2 cup mashed bananas
1 cup crushed pineapple, drained
1/2 cup dates, chopped
1/2 cup pecans, chopped
1 cup whipping cream, whipped

Place cream cheese in glass bowl and microwave on 70% power 2 to 3 minutes or until softened. Beat in syrup, lemon juice, and bananas. Stir in fruit. Fold in whipped cream. Pour in 8 inch square dish. Freeze. Let stand at room temperature for 15 minutes before serving.

Ginger Ale Molded Salad
Especially good with roast pork and ham!

2 tablespoons unflavored gelatin
1/4 cup water
1/2 cup orange juice
1/2 cup sugar
1/8 teaspoon salt
2 cups Ginger Ale
2 teaspoons lemon juice
1/2 pound Tokay grapes, seeded
1 orange, peeled and sliced
1 grapefruit, sectioned
6 slices unsweetened pineapple
3 teaspoons preserved ginger, chopped
1 cup mayonnaise

Soak gelatin in water. Place orange juice in a 4-quart measuring cup. Microwave juice on HIGH for 1 - 1 1/2 minutes or until orange juice boils. Dissolve gelatin in boiling orange juice. Add sugar, salt, gingerale and lemon juice. Chill until nearly set. Fold in fruits and ginger. Pour into an oiled 6-cup mold. Chill until set. Serve with mayonnaise.

Wilted Lettuce Salad
Great with fresh lettuce from the garden!

serves 6 to 8

5 slices bacon
3 tablespoons bacon drippings
1/4 cup cider vinegar
2 tablespoons water
1 tablespoon sugar
1/8 teaspoon pepper
1/2 teaspoon salt
1/4 teaspoon dry mustard
1 head lettuce, torn apart
4 green onions, thinly sliced

Cook bacon in a glass baking dish 4 to 5 minutes on HIGH, or until bacon is crisp. Drain bacon, crumble, and set aside. Combine remaining ingredients, except lettuce and onions, and mix well. Cook 2 to 3 minutes on HIGH or until hot. Pour hot dressings over lettuce and onions in salad bowl. Toss lightly and garnish with crumbled bacon. Serve immediately.

Two chopped hard-cooked eggs are an extra touch.

One pound of fresh spinach is a delicious substitute for the lettuce.

 If tossed salads are made in advance, break the lettuce rather than cut the lettuce to prevent browning.

Fresh Cranberry Salad

A great dish with turkey.

serves 8 to 10

1 pound cranberries, ground
1 whole orange, ground
1 cup sugar
2 (3-ounce) packages cherry gelatin
1 1/2 cups hot water
1 cup chopped pecans
1 1/2 cups chopped celery
1 (8-ounce) can crushed pineapple

Combine ground cranberries, orange and sugar. Let mixture sit overnight. Microwave water 2 minutes on HIGH and add gelatin, stirring to dissolve. When mixture starts to jell, add remaining ingredients and mix thoroughly. Pour into oiled salad mold. Refrigerate until set. Serve on lettuce leaves with mayonnaise.

June's Fresh Spinach Salad

6 slices bacon
1/2 pound mushrooms, thinly sliced
1 pound spinach, washed
½ cup green onion, sliced
2 tablespoons oil
4 tablespoons lemon juice
2 tablespoons vinegar
1 cup sliced avocado, optional
Salad tomatoes
Salt and pepper

Microwave bacon 6 to 8 minutes on HIGH. Remove bacon. Add onions to bacon fat. Microwave 1 to 2 minutes on HIGH or until onions are soft. Add oil, lemon juice and vinegar to onion mixture. Pour over spinach, mushrooms, avocado and tomatoes. Toss in crumbled bacon. Salt and pepper to taste. Serve at once.

Picnic Vegetable Salad

serves 15 to 18

1 bunch broccoli
1 (8-ounce) package fresh mushrooms
1 head cauliflower
1 (8-ounce) bottle Italian dressing

Cut broccoli into flowerets and cook 2-3 minutes on HIGH in a covered casserole dish. Cool. Slice mushrooms, break up cauliflower and put in bowl. Add cooled broccoli. Add bottle of Italian dressing. Toss thoroughly. Cool in refrigerator for several hours.

Frances's Pineapple Salad
A Tasty and Tangy salad that is great with ham or fish!

serves 6 to 8

2 tablespoons sugar
2 tablespoons flour
1 egg
1 (20-ounce) can pineapple chunks
2 cups marshmallows, cut in fourths
1/2 cup pecans

Mix sugar and flour in 4 cup glass measuring cup. Add egg to mixture and stir. Add juice from pineapple and stir. Cook 4-6 minutes on HIGH or until mixture thickens. Cool several minutes. Add marshmallows and stir until marshmallows dissolve. Add pineapple chunks and nuts. Chill thoroughly before serving. (The salad will thicken during the chilling process.)

Simply Scrumptious Strawberry Salad
Makes lots and is light and tasty!

serves 16

1 (20-ounce) can crushed pineapple
1 (6-ounce) box strawberry jello
2 cups buttermilk
1 (8-ounce) container dessert whipped topping
1/2 cup chopped nuts

Drain pineapple well, put juice in a large glass bowl. Heat juice 1 to 2 minutes on HIGH (Juice should be hot - but not boiling.) Add and dissolve jello. Cool. Add buttermilk and pineapple and put in refrigerator until mixture starts to thicken. Fold in dessert topping and nuts. Pour in large pyrex dish or several small molds.

Janie's Layered Potato Salad
A layered potato salad with mustard sauce.

6 medium potatoes, cooked and sliced
2 onions, sliced and divided in rings
3 hard boiled eggs, chopped
1 cup olives, sliced

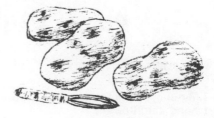

Mustard Sauce:

2/3 cup mayonnaise
1/3 cup mustard
Vinegar to taste

Microwave 6 potatoes on HIGH 15 to 18 minutes or until slightly firm. Wrap in foil or cover with a bowl 5 to 10 minutes. Cool. Peel and slice. Place a layer of potatoes, onions, eggs, and olives. Drizzle mustard sauce over vegetables. Layer and drizzle with more sauce. Chill and serve.

Mexican Salad Toss

serves 12

1 to 4 teaspoons chili powder - or to taste
1/2 teaspoon garlic salt
1 pound ground chuck
1 large head Iceberg lettuce
1 (15-ounce) can ranch style
  or kidney beans
1/2 cup celery, chopped
2 tomatoes, diced
1/4 cup olives, sliced in rings
1/2 red onion, finely chopped
1 cup sharp cheese, coarsely grated
1 (8-ounce) bottle Catalina dressing
1 (9 1/2-ounce) package corn chips, crushed

Cook ground chuck, chili powder and garlic salt on HIGH for 5 to 6 minutes. Drain and rinse chili beans. Add beans, celery, tomatoes, olives, onion, cheese and dressing to lettuce. Add drained meat. Chill for at least 1 hour. Before serving, add chips and toss.

German Potato Salad
A delicious hot salad!

serves 6 to 8

6 medium potatoes
6 slices bacon, drained
1 medium onion, sliced thinly
2 tablespoons flour
3 tablespoons sugar
1 1/2 teaspoons salt
1 teaspoon celery seed
1/2 teaspoon pepper
3/4 cup water
1/4 to 1/3 cup vinegar

Microwave potatoes on HIGH for 15 to 18 minutes and allow to stand wrapped in foil for 10 minutes. Cook bacon on HIGH for 6 to 9 minutes or until crisp. Drain bacon, reserving 1/4 cup drippings. Place onion slices in dish with drippings and cook 2 to 3 minutes. Add flour, sugar, salt, celery seed and pepper, stirring to blend. Add water and vinegar. Cook on HIGH 2 to 3 minutes. Peel and slice potatoes. Add to sauce and cook until hot. Crumble bacon and sprinkle over top. Serve hot.

Allow at least 4 to 6 hours for a mold to set. Overnight jelling is best if time is available.

When using unflavored gelatin, dissolve 1 envelope in 1/4 cup cold water. Let gelatin sit until it gels. After it gels, place it in the microwave on HIGH for 30 to 40 seconds.

Yummy Chicken Salad
A good luncheon salad!

serves 6 to 8

3 cups cooked chicken, cubed
1 can mandarin oranges, drained
1/2 cup celery, chopped
1/4 pound seedless white grapes, halved
1/4 cup slivered almonds
1/3 cup mayonnaise
1/3 cup sour cream
Salt and pepper to taste

Cook chicken in microwave. Combine chicken, celery, oranges, grapes and almonds in mixing bowl. In separate bowl blend mayonnaise and sour cream, add to chicken mixture and stir well to blend all ingredients. Chill well and serve.

Ever-Ready Coleslaw
Keeps 2 to 3 weeks in the refrigerator

serves 8 to 10

3/4 cup oil
1 cup sugar
1 cup cider vinegar
1 teaspoon mustard seeds
1 1/2 teaspoons celery seeds
1/2 teaspoon turmeric
1 teaspoon salt

Place in 1 quart container and microwave 3 to 4 minutes on HIGH or until mixture boils. Cool and pour over the following vegetables:

1 medium cabbage, chopped
1 medium green pepper, chopped
1 medium onion, chopped
1 small jar pimento, chopped

Chill and serve.

Raspberry Vinegar
Good in Salads.

1 (10-ounce) package frozen raspberries
3 or 4 (12-ounce) bottles red wine vinegar

Microwave raspberries in large glass bowl 2 to 3 minutes on HIGH. Drain off excess liquid. Rinse berries well. Place berries and vinegar back in bowl. Let stand overnight. Microwave vinegar mixture uncovered on HIGH 6 to 12 minutes so that it boils about 3 minutes. Strain vinegar, discard solids. Pour vinegar back in clean vinegar bottles. Label and store in dark place. Age 2 to 4 weeks before using. It improves with age.

Simply Delicious Vinaigrette

1/4 cup raspberry vinegar
1/2 cup olive oil
Salt and pepper to taste

Mix in bottle and shake well before serving.

Sweet and Sour Dressing

Yield: 2 cups

3/4 cup sugar
1/2 cup vinegar
1 cup oil
1 teaspoon celery seeds
1 teaspoon paprika
3/4 teaspoon salt

Combine sugar and vinegar in 4 cup glass measuring cup. Microwave 2 to 3 minutes on HIGH until mixture begins to boil. Add remaining ingredients and mix well. Chill.

Creamy Bacon Dressing
Tasty on Green Salads!

4 slices bacon
1 egg, well beaten
1/2 cup sour cream
1/4 cup cider vinegar
2 tablespoons sugar
3 green onions, thinly sliced

Cook bacon on HIGH 3 to 5 minutes or until crisp. Drain bacon and crumble. Cool bacon drippings. In a small dish, beat the egg and add the sour cream, vinegar, sugar and onion. Stir the mixture into the cool bacon drippings. Microwave 3 to 4 minutes on 70% power or until thickened, stirring every minute. Add bacon and serve.

Marinated Asparagus Salad
This is a great Italian Dressing, too!

1 pound fresh asparagus
2 onions sliced in rings
1/2 pound fresh mushrooms, sliced

Italian Dressing:

1/3 cup cider vinegar
1 tablespoon sugar
2 tablespoons lemon juice
1 teaspoon garlic salt
1/2 teaspoon dry mustard
1/2 teaspoon oregano
1/4 teaspoon basil
1 cup vegetable oil
Freshly ground black pepper

Place vinegar in 2-cup measuring cup and microwave on HIGH for 30 seconds or until vinegar is hot. Add sugar, lemon juice and spices and stir. Add oil and blend well. Cook asparagus in tightly covered dish. Microwave on HIGH 2-3 minutes. Drain and cool. Add onions and mushrooms to asparagus and cover with Italian Dressing.

Marinated Fruit Bowl

1 cantaloupe, peeled and cut in pieces
1 can Bing cherries, drained
1 cup blueberries, drained and rinsed
3 fresh peaches, peeled

Use any combination of fruits, especially fresh fruit in season.

Marinade

1/2 cup sugar
3/4 cup water
2 tablespoons fresh lime juice
Sprig of mint
1/4 teaspoon anise seed
Pinch of salt

Place marinade ingredients in 2-cup measure. Microwave on HIGH 3 1/2 minutes. Cover and steep 10 minutes. Cool. Pour over fruit and chill 2 hours or longer.

Sandwiches - General Guidelines

Sandwiches are a very versatile food item. They can go almost anywhere --picnics, snack suppers or a main dish. The microwave can make sandwiches fast, tasty and simple.

Use firm, thick slices of bread for microwave sandwiches.

Toast or day-old bread is a good choice.

Sandwich fillings and spreads should be cooked separately. The bread will become chewy and tough if cooked at the same time as the fillings.

Reheating sandwiches Is a snap in the microwave. Wrap sandwich in paper or cloth towels and reheat.

Chicken Divan Sandwiches

serves 6

3 sandwich rolls, split and toasted
6 slices cheese
3/4 pound sliced cooked chicken
1 (10-ounce) package frozen
 broccoli, thawed
3/4 cup mayonnaise
1/4 cup grated Parmesan cheese
1 teaspoon dry mustard
2 to 3 tablespoons milk
1/4 cup onion, chopped

Arrange rolls in 3-quart micro-safe dish. Place on rolls: Sliced chicken, cheese and broccoli. In a separate bowl, mix thoroughly mayonnaise, cheese, mustard, and gradually stir in milk. Spoon over sandwiches and sprinkle with onions. Microwave on HIGH 5 to 7 minutes, or until broccoli is tender. Cover with plastic wrap when cooking.

Reuben

serves 4

8 slices rye bread, toasted
4 slices Swiss cheese
4 slices corned beef (cooked)
1 cup sauerkraut, well drained
4 tablespoons Thousand Island dressing

Arrange 4 slices of bread on a paper towel. Top each slice of bread with a piece of cheese, 1 slice of corned beef, 1/4 cup sauerkraut, and 1 tablespoon dressing. Microwave 70% power 5 to 7 minutes, or until cheese starts to melt. Top with remaining slices of bread.

Pocket Bread Pizza

serves 4

4 pocket bread rounds
1 (14-ounce) jar prepared pizza sauce
1 pound Italian sausage, cooked
1 to 2 cups Mozzarella cheese, shredded

Cook Italian sausage on HIGH 5 to 6 minutes. Stir to break up sausage. Drain sausage. Place bread on paper towels. Spread pizza sauce on pocket bread rounds and place remaining ingredients on top. Microwave on 70% power 2 to 3 minutes or until cheese melts. If browning tray is available, use it to produce a crisper crust.

Sloppy Joes
This is a favorite of teens!

serves 8

1 pound ground beef
1/2 cup onion, finely chopped
1/4 cup celery, finely chopped
1/3 cup green pepper, finely chopped
1/2 teaspoon salt
1/8 teaspoon pepper
1 teaspoon Worcestershire sauce
1 cup barbecue sauce
8 hamburger buns

Place ground beef, onion, celery and green pepper in a 2-quart micro-safe dish. Microwave on HIGH 7 minutes. Drain off excess liquid. Add spices and barbecue sauce. Cook 8-10 minutes covered on 50% power. Spoon over hamburger buns.

Italian Sausage Sandwiches

serves 6

1 pound Italian sausage, sliced 1/4" thick*
1/2 sweet onion, sliced in rings
1 green pepper, cut in strips
2 tomatoes, peeled and sliced
1/4 teaspoon salt
1/4 teaspoon oregano
1/2 cup Mozzarella cheese, shredded
6 French rolls, toasted and split

Microwave Italian sausage on HIGH for 5-8 minutes. Drain well. Add vegetables and cover. Cook 3 to 4 minutes on HIGH or until tender. Stir in seasonings. Spoon on rolls. Sprinkle with cheese. Microwave on 70% power 2 to 3 minutes till cheese melts.

* Substitute ground pork or beef and flavor to taste like Italian Sausage. To do this: Sauté 2 tablespoons oil and 1 tablespoon fennel seed for 1 minute on HIGH. Let mixture set for several minutes. Strain and add oil to meat.

Simply Scrumptious
Vegetables & Fruit

Vegetables & Fruit
Vegetables

Fruits

Sauces

General Guidelines

Vegetables and fruits cooked in the microwave are Simply Scrumptious! Rapid cooking in a very small amount of water is the best way to retain nutrients and flavor.

An added bonus is the way that vegetables and fruits cooked in the microwave retain color, texture and taste. To enjoy vegetables and fruits at their peak of goodness, always begin first by selecting a quality product.

If vegetables and fruits are washed right before cooking, it is usually not necessary to add additional water.

Cover most vegetables tightly with plastic wrap to hold in moisture and speed the cooking process. Carefully uncover when removing plastic wrap to prevent burns.

Arrange whole vegetables such as potatoes, squash and beets in a ring in the microwave, allowing space between vegetables if possible.

Small pieces of vegetables cook faster and more evenly than larger ones.

Fresh vegetables will microwave faster because they contain more natural moisture.

The density of vegetables affects cooking time. Vegetables such as asparagus or broccoli should be arranged with the tougher stalks to the outside of the dish.

Always prick the skin of whole vegetables such as potatoes or squash so steam can escape.

Always allow vegetables to stand covered after removing from the microwave so the center can finish cooking without overcooking the outside.

Salt vegetables after cooking, or dissolve salt in water before adding to vegetables. This prevents dry or discolored spots.

Remember that starting temperature is important. Therefore vegetables and fruits that are chilled take longer to cook than if at room temperature.

Eggplant slices: Cut in 1/2 inch thick slices crosswise. Spread each side with soft butter. Sprinkle with salt, pepper, grated onion and lemon juice. Cook on HIGH for 30-40 seconds per slice.

Broccoli Tomato Cups
A pretty dish to serve at a dinner party.

6 servings

1 (10 ounce) package frozen
  chopped broccoli
6 medium size fresh tomatoes
2/3 cup soft bread crumbs
1/2 teaspoon salt
1/4 teaspoon pepper
2/3 cup Parmesan cheese

Place unwrapped broccoli in 1 1/2 quart dish and microwave on HIGH 5-7 minutes. Let stand covered for 2-3 minutes and drain well. Cut off the stem end of each tomato and scoop out pulp. Set aside. Combine the drained broccoli, bread crumbs, salt, pepper and half of cheese. Fill tomato cups with mixture. Add as much of the tomato pulp as needed to fill all the tomatoes. Arrange in a circle in a baking dish. Cover and microwave on HIGH 4-6 minutes. Sprinkle cheese over top and allow to stand covered several minutes before serving.

Low Calorie Summer Vegetables
Delicious!

4-6 servings

1 medium onion, sliced thinly
1 bell pepper, chopped
1 small eggplant, cubed
2 yellow squash, sliced
1 zucchini, sliced
3 tomatoes, cubed
1/4 cup cooking oil or bacon drippings
Salt and pepper to taste
1 teaspoon oregano
1/2 cup Parmesan cheese (for variety substitute sharp Cheddar)

Place all vegetables except tomatoes in baking dish and sprinkle with oregano. Cover tightly with plastic wrap. Microwave on HIGH for 6-8 minutes. Stir and check for doneness. Add salt, pepper and tomato wedges, stirring to dissolve salt. Cook 1-2 additional minutes. Remove from oven and add cheese. Cover and allow to stand for 5 minutes until cheese melts.

If using mushrooms to make shish kababs, cook in microwave until slightly limp to prevent breakage on skewer.

Acorn Squash with Parmesan

4 servings

2 acorn squash
4 tablespoons butter
4 tablespoons grated Parmesan cheese
Salt to taste and sprinkle with freshly ground black pepper

Cut squash in half lengthwise and remove strings and seeds. Place squash open side up in a baking dish. Sprinkle with salt and pepper. Add butter and cheese. Cover tightly with plastic wrap and microwave for 9-10 minutes on HIGH until squash can be easily pierced with a fork after standing 5 minutes.

Okra and Tomato Gumbo
A Southern dish that is very tasty!

2 tablespoons bacon drippings
1 medium onion, finely chopped
2 cups fresh sliced okra, or 10 ounce package frozen
2 cups tomatoes, fresh or canned
3/4 teaspoon salt
3 tablespoons sugar
1 tablespoon vinegar
Add pepper to taste

Combine all of above ingredients. Cover tightly and microwave for 10 15 minutes on HIGH. Taste to see if seasonings need adjusting. Good served over rice.

Asparagus Almondine
A taste treat in Springtime!

4-6 servings

1 pound fresh asparagus spears,
  asparagus trimmed and pared
4 tablespoons sliced almonds
2 tablespoons butter
1 tablespoon water
1/2 teaspoon seasoned salt

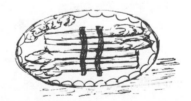

Microwave almonds and butter in small bowl or glass cup. Cook uncovered on HIGH 4-6 minutes, stirring several times. Place asparagus in glass baking dish, arranging tips in the center of dish. Add water and cover with plastic wrap. Cook on full power until almost tender, about 8 minutes. Drain. Sprinkle with toasted, buttered almonds and salt.
Variation: Follow basic cooking directions above. Melt 1/3 cup butter and add 2 tablespoons fresh lemon juice. Pour over asparagus at end of standing time. Salt and pepper to taste.

Follow basic cooking directions above, using 1/3 cup butter and fresh lemon juice. Pour over asparagus and add roasted cashew nuts.

Cream Style Corn
Southern Style

Yield 4 generous servings for corn lovers!

8-10 ears of tender corn
1/3 cup butter or bacon drippings
1/2 cup water
1/2 cup milk
2 tablespoons corn starch
Salt and pepper to taste

Cut corn from the cob halfway through kernels, and then scrape remaining corn from each ear, catching all the corn juice. Add 1/2 cup of water, along with butter or bacon drippings and place mixture in baking dish, covering tightly with plastic wrap. Cook at HIGH power 7-9 minutes, stirring once. Add corn starch to milk and blend. Add blended mixture to corn, stirring well. Cook at 70% power for 3-5 minutes, stirring once. Salt and pepper to taste. Enjoy a taste delight -- without all the stirring required in conventional cooking to prevent sticking.

Broccoli - Cauliflower Quickie

6-8 servings

2 (10 ounce) boxes frozen, chopped broccoli, thawed and drained
1 (10 ounce) package cauliflower, thawed
1 (10 ounce) can cream of celery soup
1 (4 ounce) can mushrooms
1 (8-ounce) jar Cheese Whiz
1 can French fried onion rings

Layer vegetables. Mix soup and Cheese Whiz and pour over top of vegetables. Cover with plastic wrap and microwave for 12-18 minutes on HIGH. Add onion rings and cook 1-2 additional minutes.

Broccoli Cheese Casserole

Yield 4-6 servings

2/3 cup milk
3 eggs
1/4 cup flour
1 teaspoon salt
1/4 teaspoon pepper
1 medium onion, sliced thinly
1 (10 ounce) package of chopped broccoli, thawed and drained
1 cup shredded Swiss cheese
1/2 cup cottage cheese (optional)

Blend milk, eggs, flour, salt and pepper and set aside. Alternate layers of broccoli, onions and cheese. Pour egg mixture over layers. Microwave for 10-15 minutes on 70% power. To promote even cooking after 7 minutes, gently stir the mixture toward the center.

Fresh Broccoli with Cheese Sauce

4-6 servings

1 1/2 pounds fresh broccoli spears
2 tablespoons butter
2 tablespoons flour
1 cup milk
1 cup sharp Cheddar cheese
1/2 teaspoon white pepper
Toasted sesame seeds, optional

Trim 1 inch from butt end of spears and peel if broccoli appears tough. Arrange spears with tender heads toward center of dish and cover tightly with plastic wrap. Microwave 8-12 minutes on HIGH until pieces can be pierced with fork. Cover and let stand while cheese sauce is prepared.

Melt butter and add flour, stirring until smooth. Add milk and pepper. Cook on 70% power for 4-5 minutes until thickened. Remove from oven and add grated Cheddar cheese, stirring until melted and smooth. Pour over broccoli and add toasted sesame seeds if available. Garnish with slices of tomato if desired.

Yellow Squash Casserole

6-8 servings

1 pound yellow squash, sliced
1 medium onion, chopped
1 grated carrot
1 can (10 3/4 ounce) cream of chicken soup
2 eggs
1 cup sharp Cheddar cheese, grated
1/4 cup butter
1/4 teaspoon salt
1/4 teaspoon pepper
1/2 package seasoned bread crumbs
   (Peppridge Farm)

Microwave squash, onion and grated carrot on HIGH for 6-8 minutes until tender. Drain and add soup, eggs, Cheddar cheese, butter, salt and pepper. Cover tightly with plastic wrap and cook for 6-8 minutes on HIGH. Add crumbs to the top of casserole and cook 1-2 additional minutes, uncovered.

Cabbage and Noodles Delight

4-6 servings

4 cups shredded cabbage
1 medium onion, thinly sliced
1/4 cup butter or bacon drippings
1-2 teaspoons poppy seeds
Salt and pepper to taste
2 cups cooked medium-sized egg noodles

Combine all ingredients except egg noodles in 2-quart casserole. Cook on HIGH 5-7 minutes, stirring midway through cooking time. Stir in noodles.

Acorn Squash with Cranberry
Very festive looking during the Holiday season.

4 servings

2 small acorn squash
2 tablespoons brown sugar
1/2 teaspoon cinnamon
1 (16-ounce) can whole cranberry sauce

Cut squash in half and remove seeds. Place in baking dish and sprinkle squash with brown sugar and cinnamon. Fill squash with cranberry sauce and cover tightly with plastic wrap. Cook on HIGH for 9-10 minutes, or until squash can be pierced with a fork easily.

Variations: Follow preceding recipe, substituting chopped apples for cranberry sauce and add one pat of butter to each squash half. A dash of lemon juice gives added zest!

Spinach-Stuffed Onions

8 servings

4 medium onions
1 pound fresh spinach, stems removed
2 tablespoons melted butter
1/4 cup half-and-half or evaporated milk
Salt and pepper to taste
1/2 cup Parmesan cheese

Peel onions and cut in halves horizontally. Microwave 6-8 minutes. Cool slightly, remove center of onions and dice, leaving shells intact. Wash spinach and microwave 1-2 minutes, using only water that clings to leaves. Drain and chop. (Frozen, drained spinach may also be used.) Mix chopped spinach and diced onions, adding melted butter and milk along with salt and pepper. Fill onion shells with spinach and sprinkle generously with cheese. Microwave at 70% power for 5-8 minutes until heated thoroughly.

Sweet-Sour Carrots
Hungarian Style

6 servings

1 pound fresh carrots
1/4 cup water
1 teaspoon salt
2 tablespoons butter
1/2 cup vinegar
3/4 cup sugar
1 tablespoon chopped parsley

Wash and scrape carrots, cutting them into 3 x 1/2-inch strips. Place carrots and water in dish and microwave on HIGH 8-10 minutes until slightly tender. Let stand several minutes and drain water. Add butter, vinegar and sugar and cook 3-5 minutes on HIGH. Salt to taste. Garnish with fresh parsley.

Sylvia's Corn Pudding Casserole
Century old Southern recipe.

4-6 servings

2 cups tender cut corn
1/2 cup sugar
3 eggs, well beaten
1/4 cup melted butter
1 teaspoon salt
1/2 teaspoon black pepper
1 cup milk

Mix all ingredients and pour in a casserole dish. Cover and microwave for 5 minutes on HIGH and stir. Cook 11-14 minutes on 80% power until almost set. Allow to stand 5 minutes before serving.

Variation: Substitute 2 cups of thinly sliced, fresh yellow squash and 1 medium onion for the corn and proceed.

Corn on Cob

Wrap individual ears of husked corn in plastic wrap and place in oven, cooking on HIGH 2-3 minutes per ear. Let stand 5 minutes before serving. Great, with little loss of vitamins or minerals!

If cooking 4 or more ears, it is more practical to place corn in glass baking dish and cover tightly with plastic wrap, cooking 2-3 minutes per ear and rearrange once. Butter and enjoy!

Corn in the husk is a taste delight also. Remove several outside shucks and place corn in microwave, cooking on HIGH 2-3 minutes. Remove, let stand a few minutes and pull shucks away from corn. The corn silks will follow easily!

Garden Fresh Cabbage
Simple and Delicious!

1 medium size head of cabbage
1/4 cup bacon drippings or butter

Wash and cut cabbage into uniform pieces. Cover tightly with plastic wrap and microwave for 8-10 minutes on HIGH. Remove from microwave and add seasonings. Salt and pepper to taste.

Variations: Add onion and thin slices of carrots, placing carrots around the outside edge of dish and cook as directed above.

Low-cal way: Omit bacon drippings or butter and add Lemon and Pepper seasoning (by McCormick) and salt upon completion of cooking.

Vegetables & Fruit   57

Carrot and Cheese Ring

A pretty dish served at a buffet. Fill the center with green peas and onions or carrot curls and parsley.

serves 6-8

3 cups finely shredded carrots
1/2 cup finely diced celery
1 cup finely chopped onion
1/2 cup dry bread crumbs
1 cup shredded sharp Cheddar cheese
1 1/2 cups thick white sauce (see page 69.)
3/4 teaspoon salt
1/2 teaspoon pepper
4 eggs, well beaten

Combine carrots, celery, onions, bread crumbs, cheese, white sauce, salt and pepper. Beat eggs and add to carrot mixture. Place 1 tablespoon bread crumbs in bottom of oiled 1 1/2 quart ring mold. (If mold isn't available use a smaller bowl placed in a larger round casserole dish.) Cook for 12-16 minutes on 70% power. Allow to stand 5-10 minutes before emptying out onto serving dish.

Eggplant Parmesan

6 servings

1/2 cup chopped onion
2 garlic cloves, minced
1 tablespoon butter or margarine
1 (15-ounce) can tomato sauce
1 tablespoon light brown sugar
1 teaspoon dried oregano
1/2 teaspoon dried basil
2 tablespoons milk
1 egg, beaten
1 medium eggplant, cut into
　3/4-inch thick slices
3/4 cup dried bread crumbs
1/2 cup Parmesan cheese
1 cup grated Mozzarella cheese

Sauté onion and garlic in butter in a covered casserole on HIGH for 2-3 minutes. Add tomato sauce, sugar, oregano and basil. Re-cover and cook on HIGH 3-4 minutes. Stir and reduce power to 50%. Microwave 5-7 minutes or until flavors are blended. Set sauce aside.

Blend eggs and milk together. Dip eggplant slices in egg mixture and then coat with bread crumbs. Place in 12 x 8-inch dish in a single layer, overlapping edges when needed. Cover loosely with wax paper.

Microwave on HIGH 10-15 minutes or until eggplant is fork tender, rearranging once after half the cooking time. Sprinkle with three fourths of the Mozzarella cheese. Spoon sauce over and top with remaining Parmesan and Mozzarella cheese. Cook on HIGH 1-2 minutes until cheeses melt.

Sweet-Sour Green Beans

Yield 4 servings

4 slices bacon, cut up
1 (16 ounce) can French-style green beans
1 medium onion, sliced
1/3 cup sugar
1/4 cup vinegar
1/2 teaspoon salt
1/4 teaspoon white pepper

Place bacon and onion in 1 quart casserole dish. Cover and microwave on HIGH 4-5 minutes, or until onion is tender and bacon cooked, stirring once. Add sugar, vinegar, pepper and beans. Microwave on HIGH 8-10 minutes, stirring midway through. Salt to taste.

Note: Frozen French-style beans may be substituted for canned. Simply microwave one 16-ounce package for 6-8 minutes or until hot. Drain and add • to sweet-sour mixture.

Garden Fresh Green Beans
Fresh green beans are a must.

4 servings

1/2 pound green beans (break in uniform pieces)
1 medium onion, thinly sliced
6-8 medium mushrooms, sliced
2-3 tablespoons butter
Salt to taste

Combine beans, onion, and mushroom slices. Add butter to the top of beans and cover tightly with plastic wrap. Cook for 5 minutes on HIGH stirring after 2 minutes of cooking time. Let stand 5 minutes before serving.

Onion Casserole

Great with steaks! A taste delight that is extra good with a mild onion such as Vidalia or Walla-Walla, Washington variety.

4-6 servings

3 large onions
3/4 stick butter
1/2 cup Parmesan cheese
1/2 teaspoon white pepper
1/2 teaspoon salt
Crispy buttery crackers

Peel and thinly slice onions. Place in baking dish and dot with butter. Cover with plastic wrap and microwave 3 minutes on HIGH. Stir to distribute butter and cook 5-7 additional minutes. Remove from oven and stir in cheese, salt and pepper. Cover and let stand 5 minutes while cheese melts. Add cracker crumbs to top. Enjoy!

Grated Sweet Potato Pudding

Adapted from an old Southern recipe.
Great as a dessert also.

Yield 4-6 servings

1 large raw sweet potato
1 cup sugar
1 1/4 cup milk
1/2 cup butter, melted
2 eggs, well beaten
2 teaspoons lemon flavoring
1/4 teaspoon salt

Finely grate sweet potato. Place in dish and cover tightly (a two-quart measuring container is ideal). Cook on HIGH for 5 minutes, stirring once. Add remaining ingredients and cook on HIGH 5-8 minutes, stirring once. Place in buttered baking dish and cook for 20-25 minutes on 50% power. This dish takes over 1 hour and 15 minutes if cooked conventionally.

Summer Squash Parmesan

4 servings

3 cups thinly sliced summer squash
1 cup thinly sliced onion
3 tablespoons butter or bacon drippings
1/2 teaspoon salt
1/4 teaspoon pepper
1/4 cup Parmesan cheese

Place squash, onions, butter or drippings in dish and cover tightly with plastic wrap. Cook for 5-8 minutes on HIGH until done. Add salt, pepper, and Parmesan. Allow to stand several minutes, letting cheese melt before serving.

Variation: Add 1-2 teaspoons of dried dill weed, 1 teaspoon paprika, and 2 tablespoons vinegar upon completion of cooking time.

Follow above recipe for Summer Squash Parmesan, omitting cheese for a tasty dish.

Spaghetti Squash

6 servings

Pierce rind with sharp knife several times so steam may escape. Microwave on HIGH for 10-12 minutes. Cover and let stand several minutes before cutting in half. Scoop out seeds and fibers. Use fork to remove long strands of flesh. Use a spoon to remove remaining squash down to 1/4-inch from the skin. Melt a stick of butter for 1 minute on HIGH. Sprinkle squash with 1/2 to 3/4 cup Parmesan cheese. Salt and pepper. Green onions may be used as the garnish.

Low Cal Acorn Squash
Very tasty with beef roast!

2 servings

Split in half and remove seed. Place cut side down in baking dish. Pierce outside skin several times with fork. Bake for 8-11 minutes on HIGH. Remove from microwave and add a pat of butter, salt, freshly ground black pepper and a dash of nutmeg.

Zucchini - Tomato Zip
Low in calories and fast in speed!

4 servings

2-3 medium zucchini squash, cut in 1/2-inch slices
1-2 tomatoes, quartered
1 large onion, sliced thinly
1/2 teaspoon oregano
1/4 teaspoon garlic salt
1/2 teaspoon McCormick's Lemon & Pepper
1/2 teaspoon grated Parmesan cheese
1 tablespoon butter or bacon drippings

Layer zucchini, tomatoes and onions. Sprinkle with oregano, garlic salt and lemon-pepper. Add melted butter or bacon drippings and cover with plastic wrap. Cook on HIGH for 6-8 minutes. Top with cheese. Cover and let stand for several minutes until cheese melts.

Potato and Mushroom Divine
Nutritious and Delicious.

4-6 servings

3-4 medium potatoes, cooked and sliced
2-3 tablespoons butter
1/2 pound fresh mushrooms, sliced
2 tablespoons whole wheat flour
1 cup buttermilk or milk
2 teaspoons Worcestershire sauce
1 cup sharp Cheddar cheese, grated
1 teaspoon salt
1/2 teaspoon pepper (white preferred)
2 tablespoons toasted sesame seeds
**   (microwave 3-4 minutes, stirring several times)**

Microwave potatoes and let stand while preparing other ingredients. Sauté mushrooms in butter 3-4 minutes on HIGH. Add flour, stirring to blend. Add milk and cook until thickened (3-4 minutes). Remove from microwave and add Worcestershire sauce, grated cheese, salt and pepper. Peel and layer one half of the potatoes in a greased casserole. Spoon one-half the cheese sauce over potatoes. Layer the remaining potatoes and cheese and top with sesame seeds. Cook on 80% power until heated throughout.

Cauliflower Au Gratin

6-8 servings

1 medium head cauliflower (about 1 pound)
2 tablespoons butter
2 tablespoons flour
1/4 teaspoon white pepper
1/4 teaspoon dry mustard
Salt and pepper to taste
1 cup milk
1 cup sharp Cheddar cheese, grated

Remove outer leaves from cauliflower and trim stem close to base. Wash and place cauliflower on a 9-inch pie plate. Cover with plastic wrap and microwave on HIGH 6-8 minutes. Let stand while making cheese sauce. Melt butter 1 minute on HIGH. Blend in flour and seasonings. Stir in milk and microwave on HIGH 2-3 minutes, or until thickened, stirring every minute. Add cheese and stir to blend. Place cauliflower on serving plate and pour sauce over top. Serve at once.

Quick Variation: Use 1 can Cheddar cheese soup and 1 cup of cheese such as Swiss, Cheddar or brick. Heat for 5 minutes until bubbly and pour over cauliflower.

Quick Home Style Baked Beans

6 servings

2 (16-ounce) cans pork and beans
1/3 cup ketchup
1/3 cup brown sugar
1 tablespoon dark molasses (optional)
1/2 cup minced onions or 2 tablespoons onion flakes
2 teaspoons prepared mustard
2 teaspoons Worcestershire sauce
1/2 teaspoon garlic salt
1 teaspoon Liquid Smoke (optional)
4 slices bacon

Cook bacon 4-5 minutes while gathering remaining ingredients together. Remove bacon from drippings and add onions. Cover and cook 1 1/2 - 2 minutes on HIGH. Add remaining ingredients, stirring to blend. Save bacon and crumble, adding to beans at end of cooking time. Microwave on HIGH for 3-4 minutes. Stir. Reduce power to 50% and microwave for 16-18 minutes. Allow to stand covered for 5 minutes before serving. (If a moist bean is desired, leave covered during entire cooking time.)

Baked Vidalia Onions
(or another mild large onion.)

Cut onion in half and top each with pat of butter and 1/2 beef bouillon cube. Salt and pepper. Cover and cook 1 1/2 to 2 1/2 minutes per onion, depending on size. Baste at least once during cooking.

Potatoes

General rules of thumb for successful potato baking are:

Select Russet or Idaho potatoes for a drier and fluffier baked potato.

Prick well-scrubbed potatoes and arrange at least one inch apart on a paper towel so moisture will be absorbed as potatoes cook.

Select potatoes that are uniform in size.

Use this chart as a guide for cooking potatoes:

1 med.	3-5 minutes
2 med.	5-7 1/2 min.
3 med.	7-10 min.
4 med.	10 1/2 - 12 1/2 min.

Allow sufficient standing time. Wrap potatoes in heavy kitchen towel or foil and allow to stand 5-10 minutes after cooking so potatoes will soften. If a potato is microwaved until it feels soft, it has been overcooked and will show signs of dehydration (shriveling) upon standing.

It is very hard to give specific times for potatoes because of variations in size, maturity, moisture content, type and quality. Check each potato after minimum microwaving time to see if it is beginning to feel soft. If so remove from oven, wrap and let stand as described above.

Stuffed Baked Potatoes
A good dish to prepare ahead.

4 servings

2 large baking potatoes
1/2 cup Parmesan cheese
3 tablespoons half-and-half cream,
   or sour cream
2 tablespoons butter
1/4 teaspoon salt
1/4 teaspoon white pepper

Microwave potatoes according to general rules for baked potatoes (see above). Slice potatoes in half, lengthwise, and remove center, leaving a 1/4 inch thick shell. Whip scooped out potatoes in food processor or mixer and add remaining ingredients. Stuff shells with potato mixture. Arrange in circle on serving platter and microwave on HIGH for 3-5 minutes until hot. Garnish with a dollop of sour cream and sprinkle with chives or paprika.

Boiled Whole New Potatoes

4-5 servings

6-8 small, whole new potatoes, scrubbed
3/4 cup water

Cover with plastic wrap and microwave for 6-8 minutes on HIGH until water boils. Reduce power to 50% and cook for 10-12 minutes until fork tender. Let stand 5 minutes before serving. Season as desired.

Gourmet Potatoes

A good "do ahead" dish that needs warming
only at last minute.

6-8 servings

6 medium-sized potatoes
8 ounces shredded Cheddar cheese
1/2 cup butter
1 cup sour cream
1/2 cup chopped green onion
 (tops included)
1 teaspoon salt
1/2 teaspoon pepper
 (white preferred)
Paprika

Cook unpeeled potatoes for 18-20 minutes on HIGH. Cool slightly and slice.
Melt 1/2 cup butter and add cheese, stirring to blend. Add sour cream, salt,
pepper and onions. Pour into 8 x 12-inch glass baking dish and cook uncovered for 6-8 minutes on HIGH. Saves one hour over conventional cooking.

Sweet Potato Casserole with Crunchy Top

6-8 servings

3 to 4 cups sweet potatoes
2 eggs
1/4 cup half-and-half cream, or evaporated milk
1 teaspoon vanilla
3/4 cup sugar
1/2 teaspoon salt
1/3 stick butter
TOPPING:
1/3 cup butter
3/4 cup brown sugar
1/2 cup flour
1 cup nuts (pecans or walnuts)

Cook 3 medium potatoes in microwave for 10-12 minutes. Wrap in foil for
5-10 minutes to soften. Place potatoes, eggs, milk, vanilla, sugar, salt and
butter in food processor or mixer and blend well. Pour in buttered baking
dish and microwave on HIGH 10-12 minutes, stirring once.

For topping cut butter into sugar and flour, adding nuts last. Place on top of
sweet potatoes and microwave 5-7 additional minutes on 80% power.

Frozen vegetables don't need extra water and may be cooked in their
own plastic bags. Cut an inch slice on top of bag. Add pat of butter and
cook recommended time.

Creamed Chipped Beef
on Baked Potato

Serves 2

1 jar (2 1/2 ounce) sliced dried beef
6 tablespoons boiling water
1 tablespoon minced shallots
2 tablespoons butter
2 tablespoons flour
1/2 cup chicken broth
6 tablespoons whipping cream or evaporated milk
1/4 teaspoon mustard
1/8 teaspoon ground ginger
Dash pepper sauce
1 tablespoon sherry
2 large baked potatoes with butter and parsley

Let beef stand in boiling water for five minutes. Drain and then chop. Microwave shallots in butter for 2 minutes on HIGH. Blend in flour and cook for 1 minute. Stir in chicken broth and cream and microwave for 2 minutes. Add mustard, ginger, pepper sauce and sherry. Serve over buttered potatoes.

Sweet Potato Soufflé

6 servings

3 cups cooked and mashed sweet potatoes
1/2 teaspoon salt
5 tablespoons butter, melted
1 teaspoon of "Vanilla, Butter, and Nut" flavoring
2/3 cup sugar
2 eggs
1/2 cup half-and-half cream or evaporated milk

If a food processor is available, blend all ingredients to achieve a smooth mixture. If not, use a mixer so the mixture will be smooth and free of strings. Cook in buttered baking dish for 8-10 minutes on HIGH, stirring several times. Complete cooking process in about 5 minutes on 70% power. If desired, add large marshmallows during the last 1-2 minutes of cooking for a touch children will love.

Quickie Patio Potatoes

6-8 servings

4 potatoes (about 1 1/2 pounds), thinly sliced
1 package dry onion soup mix
3 tablespoons butter
1/2 teaspoon rosemary

Melt butter in glass cup for 40 seconds on HIGH. Add rosemary. Layer potatoes in casserole dish and sprinkle soup mix over slices. Pour butter over slices. Cover tightly and cook on HIGH 10 minutes. Stir and continue cooking on HIGH until fork tender (about 5-10 minutes).

Supreme Rice Casserole
Great to serve with beef roast.

6 servings

1 stick butter, cut in chunks
1 1/3 cup uncooked Minute Rice
1 (10 3/4 ounce) can onion soup
1/3 pound fresh mushrooms sliced, or
    1 (4 ounce) can
1/2 teaspoon pepper

Combine all ingredients in baking dish. Cover tightly and microwave 5 minutes on HIGH. Stir and microwave 5 additional minutes on 50% power. Let stand several minutes before serving. Simply Scrumptious!

Rice Pilaf

6-8 servings

1 cup long grain rice (Uncle Ben preferred)
1 cup pearl barley (health food store or gourmet section of your grocery)
1/4 cup butter
8 green onions, chopped
3 cubes beef bouillon
4 cups boiling water
1 (4 ounce) can mushrooms with liquid
2 large garlic cloves, optional

Sauté rice and barley in butter 2-3 minutes. Add remaining ingredients and cover tightly. Cook on HIGH for 4-5 minutes and 16-18 minutes on 50% power.

Rice Valencia

6-8 servings

1/2 cup chopped onions
1/2 cup chopped green pepper
1/2 cup fresh mushrooms, sliced
2 garlic cloves, minced
1/2 cup butter
1/2 teaspoon paprika
1 1/2 cups long grain rice (Uncle Ben preferred)
2 1/4 cups chicken broth
1/2 cup green peas
1 1/2 teaspoons salt
1/2 teaspoon monosodium glutamate
2 tablespoons chopped pimento

Cover tightly and microwave chopped onions, pepper, mushrooms and garlic cloves in 2 tablespoons butter for 2-3 minutes on HIGH. Add paprika and rice along with chicken broth. Cook for 10 minutes on HIGH and 20-25 minutes on 50% power in a tightly covered container. Remove from oven and add remaining butter, pimento, green peas and seasonings. Let stand 5 minutes and fluff rice lightly with fork.

Brandied Peaches

Yield one quart

2 cans (1 pound-13 ounce) peach halves
1 cup granulated sugar
1/2 cup brandy, peach preferred
1/4 teaspoon almond extract

Drain peaches, saving 1 cup of juice. Set aside. Add sugar to peach juice and cook for 4-5 minutes on HIGH until heavy syrup is formed. Add brandy and almond extract. Pour over peaches and serve warm.

Fruit Compote
Good with any meat dish

6 servings

1 can pineapple chunks
1 can apricots
1 can peaches
1 can dark cherries
1/2 cup brown sugar
1 stick butter
1/2 teaspoon cinnamon
1 tablespoon cornstarch
Flavor to taste with Brandy, rum, or sherry,—spirit or flavoring. (Use the one of your choice).

Drain fruit and combine in baking dish. Make sauce by combining 1/2 cup pineapple syrup, 1/2 cup apricot syrup, 1/2 cup syrup from peaches, along with brown sugar and butter. Microwave for 5-6 minutes on HIGH, stirring to dissolve sugar. Mix cornstarch with 1/2 cup liquid from drained fruit and add to fruit to thicken. Add cinnamon and spirits or flavoring. Pour over fruit and microwave for 10-15 minutes on HIGH.

Fruit Medley
Simply scrumptious with pork or other meat dishes!

6-8 servings

1 cup pitted prunes
1 (20 ounce) can pineapple chunks, drained
1 (16 ounce) can apricot halves, drained
1 (16 ounce) can pear halves (optional)
1/2 jar orange marmalade
1/4 to 1/2 cup fruit flavored liqueur

Combine all fruit in two-quart dish. Pour liqueur and marmalade over all of mixture. Microwave for 8-10 minutes on 80% power.

Curried Fruit

10-12 servings

1 can pear halves
1 can apricot halves
1 can peach halves
2 cans pineapple chunks
1/2 pound pitted prunes, or 1 can dark, sweet cherries
1/3 cup butter
3/4 cup light brown sugar
2-3 teaspoons curry powder

Drain fruit well. Melt butter for 2 minutes. Add sugar and curry powder, stirring to blend. Place fruit in heat-proof serving dish or 1 1/2-quart casserole. Pour butter mixture over fruit and microwave 12-15 minutes on HIGH.

(Can size may vary.)

Glazed Apple Slices

Yield 4 servings

3-4 large firm apples
1 cup sugar
1 stick butter
2 tablespoons lemon juice
1 piece of stick cinnamon, if desired

Wash and core apples. Cut into slices of uniform size. Place sugar, butter, lemon juice, and cinnamon stick into 1 1/2-quart glass dish and cook on HIGH for 1 1/2 minutes. Add apples and stir to coat. Cover with plastic wrap and microwave for 6-7 minutes on HIGH, stirring once. Cook for 6-8 additional minutes at 50% power, until fork tender.

Blushing Peaches
A yummy companion to pork, beef, or lamb.
Peaches cook rosy in jelly syrup.

4-5 servings

1 can (1 pound-13 ounce) peach halves
4 tablespoons lemon juice
1/2 teaspoon grated lemon peel
1/2 cup currant jelly

Drain peach halves and reserve 1/2 cup of syrup. In a one-quart measure, place syrup, jelly and lemon juice. Cook for 6-8 minutes on HIGH until mixture begins to thicken. Pour juice over peaches in serving dish and serve warm.

Pineapple Soufflé

Delicious Served with Ham.

4-5 servings

3 eggs
2 1/2 cups crushed pineapple
1/4 cup sugar
3 tablespoons flour
2 tablespoons butter
1 tablespoon lemon juice
1/4 teaspoon salt

Place eggs in two-quart measure or bowl and beat until light. Melt butter for 45 seconds on HIGH. Add butter to eggs, along with remaining ingredients. Cook for 5 minutes on HIGH until mixture starts to thicken. Pour into 1-quart soufflé dish or pie plate and finish cooking for 5-8 minutes on 70% power.

Basic Medium White Sauce

Yield 1 cup

2 tablespoons butter
2 tablespoons flour
1/2 teaspoon salt
1/8 to 1/4 teaspoon white pepper
1 cup milk

Microwave butter on HIGH for 30-40 seconds in a one quart measuring cup or container. Stir in flour, blending to make a smooth, thin paste. Add milk, gradually stirring until smooth. Cook on HIGH 2-3 minutes, stirring every 30 seconds until sauce starts to boil. Sauce will thicken more during standing time.

VARIATIONS:

THIN WHITE SAUCE: Use 1 tablespoon each butter and flour and proceed as directed in Basic Medium White Sauce recipe.

THICK WHITE SAUCE: Increase butter and flour to 3 tablespoons each and proceed as directed in Basic Medium White Sauce recipe.

CHEESE SAUCE: Add to Basic Medium White Sauce recipe 1/4 teaspoon dry mustard, 1 teaspoon Worcestershire sauce and 1 cup (4 ounces) grated sharp Cheddar cheese. Delicious over cauliflower, broccoli, or asparagus. Also good in casseroles.

Quick cheese sauce for vegetables: Place processed cheese in measuring cup and heat for 1 minute on 80% power. Stir, and when soft enough, pour over vegetables.

Applesauce

6 servings

4-5 medium cooking apples, peeled, cored and sliced
1/2 cup water
2/3 cup sugar
1/2 teaspoon cinnamon, optional

Place apples and water in 1 1/2-quart casserole and cover with plastic wrap. Microwave on HIGH 9-11 minutes, or until tender. Stir after five minutes.

Add sugar and cinnamon to apples and mash with fork, or put in food processor for a finer texture.

Hollandaise Sauce

2 egg yolks
1/2 cup butter
1/3 teaspoon salt
1 tablespoon lemon juice
1/4 teaspoon white pepper

Microwave butter in a 2-cup glass measure for 1 minute on HIGH. Stir in egg yolks, lemon juice, salt and white pepper, blending well with wire whisk. Microwave on 70% power for 1-2 minutes, stirring every 30 seconds. Beat with a wire whisk until smooth.

Horseradish Hollandaise Sauce:

Add prepared horseradish to taste. Fold 1/2 cup whipped cream into 1 cup Hollandaise Sauce. Good over vegetables, poached eggs or fish.

Mustard - Cheese Sauce
Delicious on broccoli, brussel sprouts and cauliflower!

1/3 cup mayonnaise
1/2 teaspoon mustard
1 tablespoon dried minced onion
1 tablespoon lemon juice

Mix above ingredients together and spread on top of cooked vegetables. Sprinkle with grated Cheddar cheese and place in microwave. Cook on HIGH for 1 minute.

Simply Scrumptious
Eggs & Cheese

Eggs & Cheese

General Guidelines

Eggs are delicious when cooked in the microwave; however, they require special cooking techniques. Learning these simple techniques can give you a delicious breakfast, brunch or main dish.

Many recipes call for egg dishes to be covered with a lid, cover, plastic wrap or waxed paper to encourage more even cooking.

Eggs usually cook on 70% power.

The yolk of the egg cooks faster than the white due to the higher fat content of the yolk. When poaching an egg, remove the egg from the oven before the white is completely set or the poached egg will be tough.

NEVER hard cook an egg in the shell. The egg will burst. Eggs can be hard cooked but not in the shell. (See recipe below.)

The high fat content of cheese attracts microwave energy. Add cheese to casseroles at the end of cooking. Different varieties of cheese vary in hardness, fat, moisture content and in the way they melt. Processed cheeses melt more smoothly than dry, hard natural cheeses.

If a conventional sauce recipe calls for diced cheese, substitute shredded cheese when converting to microwave cookery. Chunks attract too much microwave energy and require excessive stirring.

Because of its high fat content, cheese melts rapidly and can become tough or stringy when overcooked. When cheese is combined with eggs, cream or milk, use a lower heat control setting to produce a smooth and creamy dish without excessive stirring.

Sauces, creamy quiches and puffy omelets are just a few of the egg and cheese dishes you can prepare in your microwave. Eggs can be attractive, nutritious and prepared so easily by using the microwave.

Hard Cooked Eggs

Never cook eggs in their shell in the microwave — they will burst. When you need hard-cooked eggs, they can be cooked in the microwave but not in the shell. Eggs cooked this way are perfect for salads, casseroles, garnishes, or sandwich fillings.

To hard-cook eggs in the microwave, separate 3 eggs and place in 2 lightly buttered bowls. Stir the yolks with a fork. Cover each bowl with plastic wrap. Cook on 50% power. Cook the yolks 45 seconds to 1 1/4 minutes and cook the whites 2 to 2 1/2 minutes. Remove when slightly underdone. Let stand, covered, for 2 to 3 minutes.

Poached Eggs Newburg

Serves 6

3 English muffins, split and toasted
6 poached eggs

Shrimp-Newberg Sauce:

1 cup Basic White Sauce (see page 79)
2 egg yolks, slightly beaten
2 tablespoons sherry
1/4 teaspoon salt
Dash paprika
1 (5-ounce) can deveined shrimp, drained
   or 5-ounce can crab meat

Prepare basic white sauce and slowly add to egg yolks, stirring constantly. Add sherry, salt, paprika and shrimp (or crab). Blend well, and microwave on 70% power 1-2 minutes.

Poach eggs following directions on page 77. Place well drained poached eggs on toasted English muffins and spoon on Shrimp-Newburg sauce. If warmer serving temperature is desired, microwave assembled muffins on 70% power until heated.

Poached eggs may be cooked in advance, refrigerated, and reheated at serving time.

ᏀᏀ ᏀᏀ ᏀᏀ ᏀᏀ ᏀᏀ

Breakfast Hot Dish

Serves: 6 to 8

1 pound sausage
1 (4 ounce) can sliced mushrooms, drained
2 1/2 cups herbed croutons
2 cups medium sharp cheese, grated
4 eggs
1 (13 ounce) can evaporated milk
1 (10 3/4 ounce) can cream of mushroom soup

Microwave the sausage on HIGH for 8 to 12 minutes or until done. Drain sausage and mushrooms in a colander. Place croutons in 3 quart, round casserole dish. Layer cheese over croutons, next mushrooms, then sausage. Beat eggs and then add milk and soup to egg mixture. Pour the egg mixture over the layered ingredients. Let stand in the refrigerator overnight. To cook, place a glass (bottom side down) in the center of the round casserole dish. Cover with plastic wrap. Microwave on 70% power for 20 to 30 minutes. Let stand 5 minutes. Parsley can be used as a garnish and a filling at the center of the dish.

74   Eggs & Cheese

Puffy Omelet

An omelet can be used with any meal ---
breakfast, dinner, or supper.

Serves: 4 to 6

6 eggs, separated
2/3 cup mayonnaise
1/4 cup water
3 tablespoons butter
1 cup cheddar cheese, grated (optional)
1 teaspoon chives, chopped (optional)

In one bowl beat egg yolks, mayonnaise and water. Set aside. In another bowl, beat egg whites until peaks form. Gently pour egg yolk mixture over egg whites and gently fold together. In a micro-safe pie plate melt the butter on HIGH for 45 seconds to 1 minute. Swirl butter to cover the pie plate. Pour the egg mixture into the pie plate. Cook on 70% power for 6 to 8 minutes, or until the eggs are soft, moist and glossy on top. Sprinkle the cheese and chives over the top of the omelet. Microwave on 70% power for 1 minute or until the cheese starts to melt. With a spatula, loosen around the edge of the omelet. Add topping if desired. Fold the omelet in half and gently slide onto a plate.

Various fillings can be used to make an omelet an any-meal dish. The plain omelet can be served at breakfast, a fruit filled omelet makes a nice luncheon omelet, and a meat filled omelet makes a delicious and nutritious supper omelet.

Scrumptious Potato Omelet with Bacon

A tasty treat that men will love. Cook and serve
in the same dish.

Serves: 2 to 3

2 slices bacon
1 medium cooked potato, diced
3 green onions, sliced
1 tablespoon pimento
1/2 teaspoon salt
2 eggs, well beaten
Dash of pepper
1 tablespoon parsley, chopped

Cook bacon on HIGH 2 to 3 minutes or until crisp in a micro-safe plate. Drain bacon. Place onions and potato in pie plate and cook on HIGH 2 to 3 minutes. Add eggs, chipped bacon, pimento, salt and pepper. Microwave on 70% power 2 to 3 minutes, or until eggs are soft and moist. Garnish with chopped parsley.

Reheating egg dishes after original cooking can cause the eggs to toughen.

Scrambled Eggs

Eggs scrambled in a microwave are quick, convenient and tasty. They will be fluffier and have more volume than conventionally cooked eggs. You can microwave and serve in the same dish. Eggs can also be scrambled in a styrofoam cup for a breakfast with a quick clean-up.

To scramble eggs in the microwave:

1. Place butter in a micro-safe dish. Microwave on HIGH for 30 seconds or until butter melts.
2. Add milk and eggs. Stir well with a fork or wire whip. Microwave on HIGH for 1/2 the cooking time.
3. Stir eggs well. Eggs around the edge of the dish are beginning to set. Stir and move eggs on the outside to the center of the dish. Microwave on HIGH the remaining time. (If cooking 4 or more eggs, stir once or twice more.)
4. Remove eggs while they are still soft and moist. Let stand 1 to 4 minutes. Stir eggs before serving.

Time Table for Scrambled Eggs

Cook: HIGH Power

Eggs	Butter	Milk	Time
1	1 tablespoon	1 tablespoon	35 - 45 seconds
2	1 tablespoon	2 tablespoons	1 1/4 - 1 3/4 minutes
4	1 tablespoon	3 tablespoons	2 - 3 minutes
6	2 tablespoons	1/4 cup	3 1/4 - 4 1/2 minutes

Brunch Eggs
A nice selection for a brunch.

Serves: 6 to 8

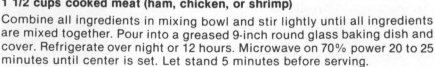

4 slices buttered and toasted bread, cubed
4 eggs, beaten
1 cup milk
Dash of Worchestershire sauce
1/2 teaspoon salt
10 ounces Cheddar cheese, grated
1 1/2 cups cooked meat (ham, chicken, or shrimp)

Combine all ingredients in mixing bowl and stir lightly until all ingredients are mixed together. Pour into a greased 9-inch round glass baking dish and cover. Refrigerate over night or 12 hours. Microwave on 70% power 20 to 25 minutes until center is set. Let stand 5 minutes before serving.

A wire wisk is an especially helpful piece of equipment to use when you cook with a microwave. A wire whisk makes sauces and puddings smooth. Lumps will disappear.

Poached Eggs

Remember 4 important steps:

1. Bring water and vinegar to a full boil on HIGH. (Vinegar helps egg white to set.)
2. Reduce power to 50% so egg will cook gently.
3. Standing time is important. (Egg white sets without overcooking yolk.) Shake cups gently once or twice during standing time. Do not remove plastic wrap.
4. Use a slotted spoon to drain egg.

To poach eggs in the microwave:

1. Measure 2 tablespoons water and 1/4 teaspoon vinegar into 6 ounce custard cup. Use one cup per egg. Cover cup with plastic wrap. Microwave on HIGH 30 to 45 seconds or until water boils.
2. Break egg into cup. Barely prick yolk with wooden pick. Cover. Microwave on 50% power 45 seconds to 1 minute 15 seconds or until most of the white is opaque but not set.
3. Let egg stand 2 to 3 minutes or until egg white is set. Shake egg gently once during standing time. Then remove cover.
4. Use a slotted spoon to remove egg. Let drain and then serve.

Time Table for Poached Eggs

Cook: 50% Power

1 egg	45 seconds to 1 minute 15 seconds
2 eggs	1 minute 10 seconds to 1 minute 30 seconds
4 eggs	2 minutes 10 seconds to 3 minutes 10 seconds
6 eggs	3 minutes 30 seconds to 4 minutes 10 seconds

Fried Eggs

Eggs can be fried in the microwave in a browning dish. They are quick and delicious.

To fry eggs in the microwave:

1. Preheat browning dish on HIGH for 2 to 4 minutes. Place 2 strips of bacon in browning dish. Microwave on HIGH 2 to 3 minutes or until bacon is crisp. Remove and drain.
2. Add 2 eggs to dish. Baste with bacon fat. Microwave on HIGH 1 - 1 1/2 minutes. Let eggs stand 2 to 3 minutes or until set.

Vinegar is used in poaching eggs to help set the egg whites.

Always use the tip of the knife or a wooden pick to break the egg yolk before cooking.

Scrambled eggs can be cooked in a styrofoam cup for quick cleanup.

Juanita's Macaroni and Cheese

Like Grandmother used to make and perhaps
still does! Children love it.

1 cup macaroni, uncooked
1/2 pound sharp cheese, shredded
3 eggs
1 (5.3 ounce) can evaporated milk or half and half
1/2 cup milk
1/2 teaspoon salt
1/2 teaspoon black pepper
1/4 cup butter

Cook macaroni conventionally while preparing other ingredients. Shred cheese and blend eggs with milk, salt, and pepper. Layer macaroni in 9 inch casserole dish alternating with cheese. Pour milk and egg mixture on top. Dot with butter. Microwave on HIGH for 5 minutes. Stir. Cook on 70% power 10 to 12 minutes—stirring once.

🦃 This dish is better if made the day before serving. The macaroni may absorb the milk. If the macaroni dish appears dry upon removing from refrigerator, add 1/4 cup milk before cooking. This dish can be browned conventionally, if desired.

Fresh Corn and Cheese Quiche

One of the best quiches you will ever eat!

Serves: 6 to 8

6 slices bacon
3 ears fresh corn
3 eggs
3/4 cup half and half or evaporated milk
1 cup Swiss cheese
2 tablespoons green pepper
1 teaspoon salt
1/8 teaspoon pepper, white preferred
1 baked 9 inch pastry shell*
Paprika
Parsley

Cook bacon on HIGH 5 to 7 minutes or until crisp. Drain and crumble. Cut corn off the cob and set aside. Beat eggs in a glass bowl. Add milk, cheese, green pepper, salt, and pepper. Microwave on 70% power for 3 to 4 minutes or until heated thoroughly. Stir well and add corn and bacon. Pour egg and corn mixture into the baked pastry shell. Microwave on 70% power for 13 to 17 minutes or until firm around edges. Center should be slightly soft. Let stand 5 minutes. Sprinkle paprika on top and garnish with parsley.

*See page 157 for pie crust recipe for microwave.

Hollandaise Sauce

A creamy sauce for fish or vegetables.

1/4 cup butter
1 tablespoon lemon juice
2 egg yolks, beaten
2 tablespoons light cream
1/2 teaspoon dry mustard
1/4 teaspoon salt
Dash Tobasco

Melt butter in a 2-cup glass measuring cup on HIGH for 1 minute. Add lemon juice, egg yolks, cream, mustard, salt and Tabasco. Stir well. Microwave on HIGH 1 minute. Beat with a wire wisk until smooth.

Basic White Sauce

So smooth and so easy with a microwave. It can be measured, mixed and cooked in the same cup.

2 tablespoons butter
2 tablespoons flour
1/4 teaspoon salt
1/8 teaspoon pepper (white pepper, preferred)
1/4 teaspoon dry mustard
1 cup milk

Melt butter in 4 cup measuring cup or glass bowl on HIGH 30 to 45 seconds. Stir in flour and seasonings until smooth. Add milk and stir well. Microwave 1 1/2 to 2 minutes on HIGH. Stir well. Microwave on HIGH an additional 1 1/2 to 2 minutes.

Variation: Cheese Sauce: Add 1/2 cup shredded cheese into White Sauce after it has been microwaved. Stir well and serve.

Artichoke Sauce

Great sauce for chicken or veal.

1/2 (15 ounce) can artichoke hearts, chopped
2 tablespoons butter
2 tablespoons flour
1/4 teaspoon salt
1/8 teaspoon pepper
1 teaspoon chicken bouillon granules
1/2 cup liquid from artichokes
1/2 cup evaporated milk

Melt butter on HIGH for 30-45 seconds. Stir in flour and seasonings until smooth. Add milk and liquid and microwave on HIGH 3-4 minutes stirring several times. Add artichokes.

Try rolled chicken breast with ham and white cheese—cooked and served on rice pilaf with artichoke sauce.

Cheese Grits — Southern Style
Quickly turns anyone into a grits lover!

1 cup quick cooking grits
3 cups water
1/2 cup butter
2 to 3 cups sharp Cheddar cheese, grated
3 eggs
1 teaspoon salt
1/2 teaspoon pepper, white preferred
1/2 teaspoon Worchestershire sauce

Cook grits, water and salt together 8-10 minutes on HIGH, stirring several times. Add butter, cheese, and seasonings stirring until mixed. Add well-beaten eggs and mix thoroughly. Pour into 8-inch square glass baking dish and cook on 80% power 10 to 12 minutes, stirring half way through.

Elegant Eggs

Serves 4

4 pastry shells, baked
1/3 cup butter
3 medium tomatoes, diced
4 green onions, and tops, thinly sliced
1/4 pound mushrooms, sliced
2 tablespoons fresh parsley
4 eggs, poached
1 cup Hollandaise Sauce (see page 70)

Poach eggs in microwave. (See page 77). Melt butter in 2-quart dish on HIGH 30 seconds. Sauté tomatoes, onions and mushrooms on 70% power for 4-6 minutes. Add parsley and stir well. Fill each pastry shell with vegetable mixture. Top with a poached egg. Spoon on Hollandaise Sauce. Garnish with paprika and parsley.

To dry herbs, place a few sprigs or a half cup on a piece of doubled paper towel. Heat 1 1/2 minutes until they crumble. Cook before storing in an air tight container.

Simply Scrumptious
Fish & Seafood

Fish & Seafood

General Guidelines

Fish is excellent microwaved. Because of its high moisture content, it cooks quickly, retains its natural flavor and can be cooked on HIGH.

It is delicate and overcooking happens quickly. Fish is done the moment it becomes opaque and the center flakes easily when lifted with a fork. Do not overcook. Cooking longer will make it dry and chewy.

The internal temperature rises about 10° during standing time. Always let stand 5 minutes before serving.

Completely thaw fish before cooking.

Arrange pieces with thicker parts toward outside of dish.

Cover the dish unless the fish itself is covered with a sauce or coating. Cook uncovered when using coatings to prevent coatings from becoming soggy, and when using sauces to prevent the sauce from becoming watery.

Quick Shrimp Curry

serves 4

1/3 cup butter
1/2 cup chopped onion
1/4 · 1/2 cup chopped green pepper
2 cloves garlic, minced
2 cups sour cream
2 teaspoons lemon juice
2 teaspoons curry powder
3/4 teaspoon salt
Dash of pepper
1/2 teaspoon ginger
Dash chili powder
3 cups cooked shrimp

Microwave butter, onion, pepper and garlic on HIGH 2-3 minutes. Stir in sour cream, lemon juice and seasonings. Add shrimp. Heat on HIGH 3-4 minutes to serving temperature. Serve over rice with desired condiments.

COOKING SHRIMP. Place 1 pound of shell-on headless shrimp in a shallow dish. Add 1/2 cup water and a dash salt. (Also add bay leaf, lemon slices or pickling spices if desired.) Cover tightly with plastic wrap. Cook on HIGH 5-6 minutes, stirring once. Drain and rinse in cold water to stop cooking. For peeled shrimp follow same procedure, but microwave on HIGH 4-5 minutes.

Baked Scallops

serves 4

1 pound sea scallops
1/4 cup butter, melted
3/4 tablespoon garlic powder
Plain bread crumbs
1/2 cup grated Parmesan cheese

Marinate scallops in butter and garlic for 1 hour or longer. Microwave in covered dish 3 1/2 - 5 minutes, stirring once during cooking to rearrange the scallops. Let stand 1 minute and test for doneness. Texture should be flaky. Cook a little longer if needed. Sprinkle with bread crumbs and cheese.

Fish Fillets with Caper Butter

serves 4

1 pound fish fillets (sole, turbot, flounder, haddock or perch)
3 tablespoons butter

Microwave butter on HIGH about 30 seconds to melt. Coat fish with butter and arrange fish with thickest portions to the outside of the dish. Cover with plastic wrap and cook on HIGH 5-7 minutes, or until fish flakes easily. Let rest about 2 minutes while you prepare the sauce.

Caper Butter Sauce:

1/4 cup butter
1/4 cup parsley, chopped
2 tablespoons capers, crushed
1 teaspoon lemon juice
1/2 teaspoon salt
Dash pepper (white preferred)

Mix sauce ingredients and microwave on HIGH 1 - 1 1/2 minutes. Drain cooking liquid from fish, pour sauce over and serve.

Other Sauces Good With Fish

ALMOND BUTTER. Combine 1/4 cup thinly sliced or slivered almonds with 1/4 cup butter and microwave on HIGH 2-3 minutes. Spoon over cooked, drained fillets.

LEMON BUTTER. Combine 2 tablespoons lemon juice, 1 tablespoon grated lemon peel (optional), 1/4 cup butter and a dash Tabasco. Microwave on HIGH 1 - 1 1/2 minutes. Spoon over cooked, drained fillets.

WHITE WINE AND GARLIC. Combine 1/2 stick butter, 2 tablespoons white wine, 1 crushed garlic clove, 1/2 teaspoon salt and dash white pepper. Microwave on HIGH 1 - 1 1/2 minutes and spoon over cooked, drained fillets.

HERBED BUTTER. Combine 1/4 cup butter and 2 teaspoons chopped fresh herbs: dill, chives, basil or parsley. Add a little wine if desired.

BACON AND GREEN ONION. Combine 2 slices cooked bacon, 1 1/2 tablespoons chopped green onion, 1 small tomato, seeded and chopped, 1/4 cup butter, 1 tablespoon lemon juice, 1/2 teaspoon salt and dash of pepper. Microwave on HIGH 1-2 minutes. Spoon over cooked, drained fillets.

Cold Paella
A favorite summer supper or luncheon dish!
Good served with a fruit salad.

serves 8-10

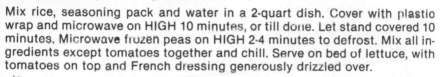

1 (10-ounce) box frozen peas
1 (6-ounce) box long grain and wild rice
2 1/2 cups water
1 jar artichoke hearts
Shrimp, cooked and peeled
(about 1 pound)
Scallions
Cherry tomatoes or tomato wedges
Bean sprouts (optional if you want crunch)

Mix rice, seasoning pack and water in a 2-quart dish. Cover with plastic wrap and microwave on HIGH 10 minutes, or till done. Let stand covered 10 minutes. Microwave frozen peas on HIGH 2-4 minutes to defrost. Mix all ingredients except tomatoes together and chill. Serve on bed of lettuce, with tomatoes on top and French dressing generously drizzled over.

Substitute canned salmon for shrimp and brown rice for wild rice for more everyday fare.

French Dressing:

6 tablespoons sugar
1 teaspoon salt
1 teaspoon celery salt
1 teaspoon dry mustard
1 tablespoon catsup
1 onion
3 tablespoons vinegar
1 cup oil
1 tablespoon lemon juice

Blend in blender.

Deviled Crab Shells

serves 6

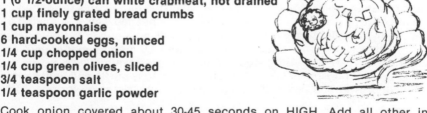

1 (6 1/2-ounce) can white crabmeat, not drained
1 cup finely grated bread crumbs
1 cup mayonnaise
6 hard-cooked eggs, minced
1/4 cup chopped onion
1/4 cup green olives, sliced
3/4 teaspoon salt
1/4 teaspoon garlic powder

Cook onion covered about 30-45 seconds on HIGH. Add all other ingredients. Mix and place in 6 scallop shells or ramekins. Sprinkle with additional bread crumbs and a small pat of butter on top. Microwave at 70% power 2-4 minutes.

Baked Haddock or Sole

serves 4

1 pound fish
Salt and pepper
Grated lemon peel, to taste
2 tablespoons lemon juice
2 tablespoons chopped green onion
1 tablespoon chopped parsley
1 teaspoon seasoned salt
1/2 cup mayonnaise

Arrange fish in baking dish with thickest portions to the outside. Mix remaining ingredients and spread on fish. Microwave uncovered on HIGH 5-7 minutes or until done. Garnish with parsley and lemon peel.

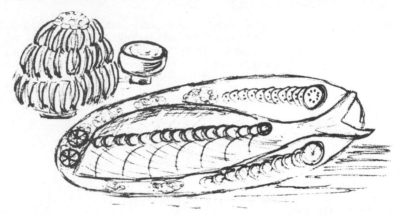

Poached and Steamed Fish

Microwave-poached and microwave-steamed fish are tender and moist because of lack of dry heat. Poaching and steaming produce superior results. Conventionally, fish is poached in a liquid, which flavors the fish and keeps it moist. When converting a conventional recipe to microwave, reduce the liquid. Water, white wine, clam juice or chicken broth may be used.

Conventional directions call for wrapping a whole fish in cheese cloth to keep it moist and to hold the fish together when it is turned; this is not needed in microwaving. Only a covering on the dish is needed. Cover, allowing a steam vent, and microwave on HIGH 8-11 minutes per pound for whole fish, 5-7 minutes per pound for thick fish steaks, and 2-6 minutes per pound for thinner cuts. When converting steamed fish recipes to microwave, no liquid needs to be added. The moisture content of the fish is sufficient. Just cover with plastic wrap and follow the same microwaving times as for poached fish.

🍲 Whole fish may be baked, steamed or poached, but shielding with foil may be needed on the tail and thin parts to prevent overcooking (if your oven permits use of metal). Cook covered 6-15 minutes per pound.

Crab and Artichoke Casserole

serves 4-6

3 tablespoons butter
3 tablespoons flour
1 1/2 cups milk
1 teaspoon salt
1/8 teaspoon pepper
1/2 teaspoon Worcestershire sauce
1/2 cup Cheddar cheese
1/3 cup Parmesan cheese
Dry mustard to taste
Hot sauce to taste
4 hard-cooked eggs, chopped
1 (15-ounce) can artichoke hearts
2 cups crab meat
1/4 cup or more Parmesan cheese

Microwave butter and flour on HIGH about 2-3 minutes. Gradually add milk, stirring constantly. Add remaining ingredients except 1/2 cup Cheddar cheese. Pour into 1 1/2-quart casserole. Microwave on 70% power about 5-10 minutes to thicken. Sprinkle top with 1/2 cup Cheddar cheese. Cook on HIGH about 1-2 minutes longer.

Rock Eagle Seafood Casserole

serves 10

8 ounces crab meat
8 ounces lobster meat (we substitute
  white chicken meat, chopped)
1 pound shrimp, cooked and shelled
1 cup mayonnaise
1/4 cup chopped green pepper
2 tablespoons chopped onion
1/4 teaspoon salt
1 1/2 teaspoons Worcestershire sauce
5-6 ounces potato chips
Paprika

Combine all ingredients except chips and paprika. Spread in casserole dish, cover. Cook on HIGH 5-6 minutes to thoroughly heat, stirring several times. Spread crushed potato chips over casserole and sprinkle generously with paprika. Microwave uncovered on HIGH 1-2 minutes longer, without stirring.

Whole lobster or lobster tails can be microwave-steamed in a few minutes. Put 1/2 cup water in a casserole and microwave on HIGH to boiling. Add lobster, cover and microwave on HIGH till the shell turns red and the meat is white and tender. Overcooking can toughen the meat.

Sherried Crab

serves 8-10

3 tablespoons butter
3 tablespoons flour
2 cups milk (or half-and-half)
1 (4 ounce) jar pimento, chopped
3/4 green pepper, finely chopped
1 1/2 cups tiny green peas (frozen preferred)
1 teaspoon sherry extract, or to taste
Salt and pepper
2 (6 1/2 ounce) cans crab meat
Grated Romano or Parmesan cheese
Paprika

Cook butter and green pepper about 2-3 minutes on HIGH till pepper is soft. Stir in flour. Add milk, pimento and sherry extract. Microwave about 4-5 minutes on HIGH till mixture starts to boil. Add crab and peas and sprinkle with cheese and paprika. Microwave on HIGH till bubbly, 2-3 minutes. Serve on toasted rosettes, timbales, pastry shells or puff pastry.

Baked Salmon Steaks

serves 4

4 (1-inch thick) salmon steaks
2 tablespoons butter
2 tablespoons lemon juice
Salt and pepper
1 small onion, sliced
Paprika

Melt butter on HIGH about 30 seconds. Add lemon juice, salt, and pepper. Pour over salmon. Top with onion slices and cook on HIGH 5-6 minutes. Let stand 5 minutes. Serve with lemon wedges.

Shrimp Scampi

serves 4

2 cups cooked shrimp
1 clove garlic
3 tablespoons parsley, finely chopped
1/4 teaspoon paprika
1 stick butter
1/4 cup dry sherry
2 teaspoons chopped shallots
5 tablespoons lemon juice
Salt and pepper to taste

Combine all ingredients except shrimp and microwave on HIGH 1 1/2 - 2 1/2 minutes to melt butter and cook shallots. Stir in shrimp. Let sit about 10 minutes to blend flavors. Microwave on HIGH 1-2 minutes to serving temperature. Good served with wild rice.

Hot Tuna Salad
Quick Supper Dish.

serves 6

2 cups sliced potatoes or (1-pound) can white potatoes, drained and sliced
1 (7-ounce) can tuna, drained
1 tablespoon dehydrated green pepper flakes
1/2 cup each chopped celery and olives
1 apple, peeled and chopped (optional)
1/2 teaspoon dried basil
1 tablespoon lemon juice
1/2 teaspoon salt
1/2 cup French dressing
1 (3 1/2-ounce) can French fried onion rings

If using fresh potatoes, cook potatoes, apple and celery covered with 1/2 cup water on HIGH 5-7 minutes, or until tender. If using canned potatoes, cook celery and apple on HIGH about 1-2 minutes. Add all other ingredients except onion rings to potato mixture and microwave on HIGH about 3-5 minutes, until thoroughly heated. Stir in onion rings and let stand 2 minutes.

Flounder Parmesan

serves 4

1 pound fillet of flounder
1/2 cup sour cream
2 tablespoons grated
    Parmesan cheese
1 teaspoon lemon juice
1 tablespoon grated onion
1/2 teaspoon salt
Dash hot pepper sauce
Paprika
Chopped parsley

Cut fish into serving size portions. Arrange fillets in baking dish with thickest portions to the outside. Mix remaining ingredients except paprika and parsley; spread mixture on fish; sprinkle with paprika. Cook uncovered on HIGH 5-7 minutes until done. Garnish with parsley.

A lingering fish odor is usually not a problem in the microwave oven since spatters do not bake on. However if your oven does need "freshening" after cooking fish, place half a lemon in a custard cup in the oven. Microwave on HIGH for 1½-2 minutes. Or wipe the oven interior with baking soda on a damp cloth.

Defrosting fish. Fish defrosts very quickly in the microwave. As a rule, allow 2-3 minutes per pound of boneless fish on the defrost setting. Separate the pieces as soon as possible. Remove fish from the oven while it is still a little icy and complete defrosting under cold running water.

Seafood Sauces

Rèmoulade Dressing

Makes 2 1/4 cups

2 cups mayonnaise
1/2 teaspoon chervil
1/2 teaspoon tarragon
1-2 tablespoons chopped green onion tops
1/2 teaspoon dry mustard
1/2 teaspoon ground red pepper
1/4 - 1/2 teaspoon Tabasco sauce
1 1/2 - 2 teaspoons anchovy paste
1 teaspoon chopped sweet pickle or relish
1/4 cup prepared horseradish
1 teaspoon capers (Always crush capers for best flavor)
1 teaspoon paprika
1/2 teaspoon cayenne
1/4 - 1/2 teaspoon parsley flakes

Combine ingredients and refrigerate. Sauce will keep as long as mayonnaise. Serve over shrimp or crab on a bed of lettuce. (See directions for cooking shrimp on page 83.)

Shrimp Sauce

4 egg yolks (raw)
1 quart salad oil
1 teaspoon salt
1/2 teaspoon hot sauce
Juice of 2 lemons
1 tablespoon vinegar
1 (16-ounce) bottle tomato catsup

Beat egg yolks. In a separate bowl, combine salt, hot sauce, lemon juice and vinegar. Gradually add oil and vinegar mixture to eggs. Mix well and add catsup. Keeps in refrigerator several weeks.

COCKTAIL SAUCE: 1 cup good mayonnaise, 1 tablespoon lemon juice, 3 tablespoons tomato catsup, 3 tablespoons chili sauce, 2 tablespoons horseradish, 2 tablespoons whipped cream. Combine these ingredients and season with hot sauce, mace, celery salt, cayenne or nutmeg to taste. Good with shrimp or crab.

COCKTAIL SAUCE II: 4 tablespoons chili sauce, 2 teaspoons lemon juice, 1 1/2 teaspoons Worcestershire, 1 - 1 1/2 teaspoons grated horseradish, salt and red pepper to taste. Combine ingredients. Good with oysters.

TARTARE SAUCE: 1 cup mayonnaise, 3 tablespoons chopped   pickle, 1 tablespoon chopped parsley, 1 tablespoon chopped capers, 2 tablespoons chopped stuffed olives, 1 teaspoon chopped onion. Combine ingredients and store in refrigerator.

Simply Scrumptious
Poultry

Poultry

General Guidelines

Poultry is an all time favorite in the meat category, being economical, low in calories and versatile. When prepared in the microwave it will be very juicy and flavorful. Listed below are some guidelines to follow when microwaving poultry:

All poultry should be completely thawed before cooking is started. Defrost on 30% power for 6-9 minutes per pound. Then let stand 5 minutes, or until the meat feels soft but still cold.

When cooking, choose a large utensil so the cut-up meat does not overlap, with the larger, thicker pieces to the outside of the dish. After initial cooking, rearrange the pieces so the less cooked parts are on the outside of the utensil. When cooking chicken pieces with a coating or browning agent, do not turn the pieces over. When cooking with a sauce, turn pieces over halfway through cooking.

Turn the whole bird at least once during microwaving; cook the breast side down during the first half of cooking time, turning the breast side up during the last half.

Allow standing time to finish cooking.

Test for doneness using conventional methods. The legs should rotate and move freely at the joints, meat should be fork tender, with juices clear and showing no pinkish tint.

For best cooking results, select a turkey that weighs no more than 12 to 14 pounds. If your oven cavity is small, carefully center the turkey in the oven, making sure there are 3 inches of space between the turkey and oven walls. It is usually necessary to shield the wings and legs with a small piece of foil to prevent overcooking.

For crispy skin, after microwaving place poultry in a 375ºF. oven and cook until skin becomes crisp and brown.

Cornish hens and chicken pieces microwave so fast that they do not have time to become crisp and brown. Use a browning agent, crumb coat or cook with a sauce.

Whole Turkey

10 to 11 Pound Turkey

Place turkey, breast side down in a micro-safe dish. (A bacon or meat rack placed in a casserole dish works well.) Turkey should cook 12 to 15 minutes per pound. Divide the cooking time in half. Microwave on HIGH for 10 to 12 minutes. Reduce power to 50% and cook remainder of first half of time. Turn breast side up. Microwave remaining time. Tent turkey with foil and let turkey stand 20 to 25 minutes or until internal temperature reaches 170°F.

Note: Shield turkey with foil as needed, if permitted in your microwave. Check instruction book.

Marinated Turkey

2 1/2 pound boneless turkey roast
2 tablespoons Liquid Smoke
1 teaspoon thyme
1/8 teaspoon cayenne pepper
1 tablespoon lemon juice

Mix Liquid Smoke, thyme, cayenne pepper, and lemon juice in a large plastic bag. Add turkey roast to bag and secure. Let roast set overnight. Turn roast several times during marinating. Remove roast from bag and place on a baking rack. Microwave on HIGH 5 minutes. Turn turkey roast over. Continue to cook on 50% power 25 to 35 minutes. Let stand 10 to 20 minutes, tented with foil. (Meatiest portions should reach 170ºF. when tested with a meat thermometer.)

Chicken Coatings

Coatings can be put on chicken to give an attractive appearance or to enhance the flavor. These recipes will coat 2 1/2 to 3 pounds of chicken pieces.

Combine all coating ingredients in a shallow dish or on wax paper. Melt butter in a shallow micro-safe dish. Add eggs and beat well. Dip chicken in egg mixture and then in coating mixture.

CORN MEAL COATING

3/4 cup corn meal
2 tablespoons celery seeds
2 tablespoons paprika

DIP

3 tablespoons butter
2 eggs

EXTRA CRISP COATING

2 (3-ounce) cans fried onion rings, crushed

DIP

1 tablespoon butter
2 eggs
1 tablespoon milk

CHEESE AND CRUNCHY

1 cup corn flake crumbs or
   or bread crumbs
1/3 cup Parmesan cheese
1 tablespoon parsley flakes
1 teaspoon garlic salt
dash pepper

DIP

1/3 cup butter
2 eggs

Place chicken on micro-safe dish and place meaty pieces of chicken to outside of dish. Microwave on HIGH 8-10 minutes and reduce to 10% power for 15-18 minutes. Let stand 5 minutes.

Chicken Cordon Bleu

An elegant chicken dish with ham and Swiss cheese.

6 medium whole chicken breasts, boned
1 (8-ounce) package Swiss cheese slices
1 (8-ounce) package sliced cooked ham
3 tablespoons all-purpose flour
1 teaspoon paprika
6 tablespoons butter, melted
1/2 cup dry white wine
1 chicken bouillon cube
1 tablespoon cornstarch
1 cup heavy or whipping cream

Place chicken breast between wax paper. Pound to flatten to 1/4 inch thickness. Place Swiss cheese and ham on chicken. Roll chicken breast over filling and fasten edges with tooth picks. Mix flour and paprika on waxed paper and coat chicken. Place chicken in 2-quart micro-safe dish. Melt butter on HIGH 45 seconds or until melted. Drizzle butter over chicken. Cook 5 minutes on HIGH. Add wine and bouillon. Microwave on 70% power for 25-30 minutes or until tender. Blend cornstarch and cream and gradually add to chicken. Cook on 70% power for 2 to 3 minutes or until thickened.

Turkey or Chicken Divan

A great way to use left-over chicken or turkey!

4 tablespoons butter
3 tablespoons flour
1 cup chicken stock (homemade is best)
1 cup milk
1/2 cup mayonnaise
1/2 cup whipping cream
1/2 teaspoon curry powder
2 teaspoons Worchestershire sauce

Make a white sauce by microwaving butter on HIGH for 1 minute or until melted. Stir in flour. Add chicken stock and blend well. Microwave on 70% power 4 to 5 minutes or until thickened. Whip in remaining ingredients.

Pour Sauce Over:

1 bunch broccoli, cooked and divided into flowerets
4 servings chicken or turkey, cooked and sliced
1/3 cup Parmesan cheese, grated

Heat casserole on 70% power for 6 to 10 minutes or until bubbly. Top with freshly grated Parmesan cheese.

When you are in a hurry, cook the chicken or turkey in the microwave for the first half of cooking time and then finish the cooking process on the grill.

Chinese Barbecued Chicken

1/4 cup soy sauce
1 tablespoon vegetable oil
3 tablespoons brown sugar
1 teaspoon dry mustard
1/2 teaspoon ground ginger
1 garlic clove, minced
2 1/2 to 3 pounds chicken, skin removed

Mix first 6 ingredients in 2 quart micro-safe dish. Add chicken and coat with sauce mixture. Let chicken marinate in sauce for at least 30 minutes. Microwave on HIGH 8 to 10 minutes. Turn chicken over and baste with sauce. Continue to cook 13 to 16 minutes on 70% power or until chicken is tender.

*This recipe works well to cook in microwave and then finish on grill.

Cheesy Chicken

2 1/2 to 3 pounds chicken, cut up
Garlic salt
Paprika
1/2 cup Parmesan cheese, grated
2 cups seasoned bread crumbs
3 eggs, well beaten
3 tablespoons milk
1/2 cup butter, melted

Season chicken with paprika and garlic salt. Beat eggs and milk in shallow bowl. Place bread crumbs and cheese in shallow bowl and blend. Coat chicken first in egg mixture and then in bread crumb mixture. Place chicken in micro-safe dish with meaty portions to outside of dish. Drizzle butter over chicken and sprinkle any remaining bread crumbs. Cover with wax paper and microwave on high 5-8 minutes. Continue to cook on 70% power 15-18 minutes or until done. Let stand 5 minutes.

Chicken in a Wink

Serves: 4 to 6

3 pounds chicken breast
1 (10 3/4 ounce) can cream of mushroom soup
1 (10 3/4 ounce) can cream of chicken soup
1 package dry onion soup mix
1/2 cup sherry
1 garlic clove, minced
1/2 cup toasted, slivered almonds
3/4 cup sour cream

Place chicken in a micro-safe dish with the meatiest parts to the outside of the dish. Combine the 3 soups, sherry, and garlic in a bowl. Coat chicken with sauce. Cover with plastic wrap. Cook 10 to 12 minutes on HIGH. Rearrange less cooked portions to outside. Cook on 70% power 15 to 18 minutes or until chicken is fork tender. Allow to stand covered 10 minutes. Remove chicken and add 3/4 cup sour cream to gravy. Garnish with toasted almonds.

Hot Turkey Salad
Rich and Delicious!

3 cups chopped turkey (cooked)
2 cups chopped celery
1 cup mayonnaise
2 tablespoons diced onion
1 (10 3/4 ounce) can cream of chicken soup
1 (4 ounce) jar pimento
1 scant tablespoon lemon juice
Salt and pepper to taste

Mix all ingredients together and place in a 13 x 9 x 2 inch micro-safe dish. Top casserole with:

1/3 cup melted butter
1 cup bread crumbs

Microwave on 70% power 10 to 12 minutes or until casserole is hot and bubbly.

Chicken Ratatouille
A Prize-winning Recipe.

4 servings

1/4 cup oil
2 whole chicken breasts (boned, skinned and thinly sliced)
2 small zucchini, thinly sliced
1 small eggplant (peeled and cut in 1-inch cubes)
1 large onion, thinly sliced
1 teaspoon dried parsley
1 medium green pepper (seeded and cut in 1-inch cubes)
1/2 pound mushrooms, sliced
1 pound tomatoes (peeled and cut in wedges)
2 garlic cloves, minced
2 teaspoons monosodium glutamate
1 teaspoon salt
1 teaspoon basil
1/2 teaspoon black pepper

Heat oil in 2-quart casserole on 80% power for 2 minutes. Add chicken and sauté on HIGH for 4-6 minutes. Add zucchini, eggplant, onion, green pepper, mushrooms and spices and cover tightly. Microwave on HIGH 5-8 minutes or until chicken is done and vegetables are tender crisp. Add tomatoes and stir gently. Microwave on 50% power 2-3 minutes. Serve with rice.

Cook a whole chicken or turkey—or turkey breast—with the breast side down for the first half of the cooking time and then turn breast side up for the remainder of the time.

Be sure the poultry items are thoroughly defrosted before they are cooked in the microwave.

Chicken Breast Parmesan

1 (8-ounce) can tomato sauce
2 garlic cloves, minced
1/2 teaspoon basil
1/2 teaspoon oregano
1/2 teaspoon salt
1/2 cup corn flakes, crushed
1/3 cup grated Parmesan cheese
2 teaspoons sesame seeds
1 teaspoon parsley flakes
6 large chicken breasts, spiit and skin removed
1 egg, beaten
1 teaspoon water
2/3 cup Mozzarella cheese

In a small shallow bowl, beat egg and add water. Set aside. Combine tomato sauce, garlic, basil, oregano, and salt in a 2-cup measuring cup. Cover with plastic wrap and microwave on HIGH for 1 1/2 - 2 1/2 minutes. Stir and microwave 3 to 5 minutes at 50% power. Remove and set aside. Mix cornflake crumbs, Parmesan cheese, sesame seeds, and parsley flakes. Dip chicken in egg mixture and then in crumbs. Place in 12 x 8-inch baking dish. Cook on HIGH 5-8 minutes. Continue to microwave at 70% power for 10-13 minutes or until chicken is done. Pour tomato sauce mixture over chicken. Sprinkle Mozzarella cheese over chicken. Cook on 70% power for 2 to 4 minutes or until cheese melts.

Baked Chicken with Artichokes
One of the tastiest chicken dishes you will ever eat!!

1/4 pound mushrooms, thinly sliced
1 onion, finely chopped
2 garlic cloves, finely chopped
3 pounds meaty chicken pieces
1/3 cup flour
1 1/2 teaspoons salt
1 1/2 teaspoons paprika
1/2 teaspoon dried rosemary
1/4 teaspoon white pepper
1/2 cup chicken broth
1/4 cup dry sherry
1 (6-ounce) can artichoke hearts, drained

Mix mushrooms, onion, and garlic in micro-safe dish. Mix flour, salt, paprika, rosemary, and white pepper. Coat chicken in flour mixture. Place chicken on top of vegetables. Pour chicken broth and sherry over chicken and vegetables. Cook on HIGH for 10 minutes. Move chicken pieces on outside of dish to center and center pieces to outside. Continue to cook on 70% power 12 to 15 minutes or until chicken is done. Add artichoke hearts and gently stir into chicken dish. Bake on 70% power 3 to 5 minutes. Let stand 5 minutes.

🐓 To help with counting calories, skin the chicken or turkey before cooking.

Chicken a la Fruit

A delicious and colorful chicken dish
to please any gourmet!

1/4 cup butter, melted
1 (12-ounce) can frozen orange juice concentrate
2 garlic cloves, minced
1/3 cup catsup
1/4 cup lemon juice
2 tablespoons soy sauce
1 teaspoon allspice
1/4 teaspoon ginger
1/2 teaspoon salt
6 whole chicken breasts, split and skinned
Juice of a whole lemon
2 bananas, peeled and sliced
1 (11-ounce) can mandarian orange sections, drained
1 (3-ounce) jar maraschino cherries, drained

Mix first nine ingredients in a small mixing bowl and stir well. Place chicken in 3 quart baking dish. Pour orange juice mixture over the chicken and cover. Place in refrigerator and let chicken set in mixture several hours to overnight. Drain marinade from chicken and reserve. Cook chicken on HIGH 10 minutes. Baste with marinade and continue cooking on 70% power 12-15 minutes or until done. Place bananas in lemon juice and stir well to coat. Drain bananas adding orange sections and cherries. Add fruit mixture to chicken and cook on 70% power 2-3 minutes longer.

Moo Goo Gai Pan

A tasty chicken dish with an Oriental flair.

4 chicken breasts
2 tablespoons oil
3 ounces snow peas
1/2 cup mushrooms, thinly sliced
2 tablespoons green onions, thinly sliced
1/2 cup water chestnuts
1 cup water
2 teaspoons instant chicken granules
2 tablespoons soy sauce
2 teaspoons cornstarch
1/2 teaspoon ground ginger
1/8 teaspoon pepper

Skin and bone chicken and cut into bite-size pieces. Mix chicken and oil in glass casserole. Microwave on HIGH 8 to 10 minutes. Let stand covered 5 minutes. Add peas, mushrooms, green onion, and water chestnuts. Microwave on HIGH 4 to 5 minutes. Remove from microwave.

In glass bowl place water, chicken granules, cornstarch, soy sauce, and spices. Cook on HIGH 3 minutes or until thickened. Stir every minute. Pour over chicken and stir well. Serve with rice.

Honey and Sesame Chicken
Try this dish!

Serves: 4 to 6

1/2 cup butter
1/2 cup honey
1/4 cup prepared mustard
1/4 cup lemon juice
2 1/2 to 3 pounds chicken, cut-up
Salt to taste
1/4 cup toasted sesame seeds

Melt butter on 70% power for 1 to 1 1/2 minutes. Add honey, lemon juice, and mustard, and stir well. Place chicken in 13 x 9 x 2 micro-safe dish. Meaty portions of chicken should be placed to outside of dish. Pour honey mixture over chicken. Refrigerate several hours. Microwave on HIGH 12 minutes. Rearrange chicken so less cooked portions are to outside of dish. Baste chicken with drippings. Microwave on 70% power for 10 to 12 minutes or until chicken is fork tender. Let stand 5 minutes covered. Sprinkle toasted sesame seeds on chicken and serve.

Turkey Breast
Juicy and Delicious!

5 to 6 pound turkey breast

Place a turkey breast, breast side down in a micro-safe dish. (A bacon or meat rack placed in a casserole dish works well.) Divide the cooking time in half. Microwave on HIGH for 5 to 8 minutes. Reduce to 50% power and cook remainder of the first half of time. Turn breast side up. Microwave remaining time or until internal temperature is 170°F. Tent turkey with foil and let turkey stand 10 to 15 minutes.

Note: Total cooking time is 11 to 15 minutes per pound.

TIPS TO TEST DONENESS OF TURKEY:

1. With a probe, temperature should reach 170° F. Check temperature several places in the turkey.
2. Juices should run clear with no hint of pink.
3. Legs should move freely.
4. Meat should be done with no hint of pink.

To test poultry for doneness: Check meat next to the bone. The meat should be fork-tender. The juices should be clear with no hint of pink.

Simply Scrumptious
Meats

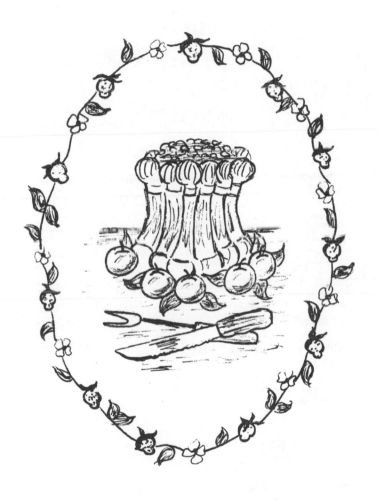

Meats

General Guidelines

Successful beef and pork cookery requires a higher level of skill and more attention—whether cooking conventionally or microwaving. Meats cooked in the microwave can be juicy and tender if properly cooked. Meats cooked more than 15-20 minutes brown nicely in their own juices.

Beef and pork are America's favorite meats. You will find that if you select meat wisely, store it properly and choose appropriate cooking methods, microwaved beef and pork will be more flavorful, tender and juicy than conventionally cooked meat.

Meat Characteristics when Microwaving:

Shape of Roast: Evenly shaped meats cook more evenly. Irregular shapes cook faster in thin areas. Shielding this area with foil (if your oven owner's manual permits) gives more even cooking.

Bone: Bones conduct heat. When a bone is on one side of a roast, that side cooks first. Boneless cuts of meat cook slower, but more evenly. Center bones surrounded by more than 1 inch of meat have little effect on cooking.

Less Tender Cuts: As in conventional cooking, less tender cuts of meat need moist methods of cooking, while tender cuts must be dry roasted or grilled. In the microwave, cover less tender cuts tightly and reduce the power level to 50% or lower for longer, slower cooking. Use less liquid than you would conventionally since little evaporation takes place. Less tender cuts may be cooked in the microwave clay pot or crock pot.

Fat: As in conventional cooking, well-marbled meat is more tender than very lean meat. Even layers of fat on the outside of the meat help it microwave evenly. If the fat cover is heavy on one area, the meat next to it will cook faster and can easily over-cook. It may be necessary to trim fat evenly for better results.

Drippings: For more efficient cooking, and to help prevent splatters, remove drippings at intervals during cooking because drippings absorb microwave energy away from lean meat and this slows the cooking process.

Turning or Rotating: Turning of food is more important with larger cuts of meat. Rotating, however, is not necessary in many ovens. Follow manufacturer's directions for this procedure.

Standing Time: This is extremely important since meat continues to cook and tenderize. Do not test for doneness until after completing standing time. The internal temperature will rise at least 10-15 degrees during this period. If you decide the meat is not done, it may be microwaved longer after standing. Make a tent of foil, shiny side down, over the meat during standing time to hold in moisture and complete the cooking process. If meat is wrapped tightly, however, it will have a steamed flavor.

Beef Roast in Rock Salt

Rock salt completely encases beef roast, holding in moisture so it does not become tough and dried out. Best cooked to rare or medium.

8-10 servings

4-5 pound beef roast (eye of round, sirloin or chuck)
6-9 garlic buds, cut in half
2 stalks of celery, cut in 3 inch slices
1 medium onion, sliced
5 pound box rock salt
1 large (14 x 20-inch) Brown-In Bag
Freshly ground black pepper
Kitchen Bouquet Sauce

Blot roast well with paper towels. Cut 12 to 14 slits in roast, dividing between all four sides. Place a garlic half in each slit. Rub Kitchen Bouquet Sauce and pepper on roast. Place in Brown-In-Bag in a large microwave-safe dish, such as a 3-quart casserole. Pour 1 1/2 to 2 inches of rock salt in bottom of bag. Place celery and onion slices on top of salt. Pour in remainder of salt and pat salt in place, being sure there is 1½-2 inches of salt on all sides. Use a string or rubber band to close the top of Brown-In-Bag. Pull the bag tight so the salt will stay in place. Make 3 slits in top of bag for steam to escape. Microwave for 10 minutes on HIGH, and 45-60 minutes on 30% power. If available, use probe to check temperature, cooking to 125°F for rare and 145°F for medium. It is best to remove at 125°F because the hot rock salt will still continue to cook the meat.

When roast is done, let stand 10 minutes. Scrape salt from roast, being careful, because salt will be very hot. Use a vegetable brush to remove remaining salt from roast. It will not have a salty taste if salt is carefully brushed off. Even tougher cuts of meat such as chuck roast will be tender, moist, and delicious.

Instead of using Kitchen Bouquet brushed on roast, marinate in Dr. Jim's Marinade recipe found on page 114 for a delicious, flavored roast.

Veal Marsala

Serves 2

1/2 pound veal, sliced
Salt and pepper to taste
1 1/2 cups fresh mushrooms
3/4 cup chopped green onions
1/2 cup butter
1/4 cup sherry
1/2 cup Marsala wine
Chopped parsley

Microwave butter for 45-60 seconds on HIGH until melted. Add veal and sauté on HIGH for 30 seconds. Turn over and cook 30 seconds. Add mushrooms and green onion. Sauté covered for 2-3 minutes on HIGH. Add sherry and Marsala and microwave about 2 minutes on HIGH, just to heat. Sprinkle with parsley and serve over wild rice. Delicious!

Crown Roast of Pork
With Rice Stuffing

A Crown Roast makes a dramatic party presentation!

8 servings

6-7 pound crown roast of pork
(Order crown roast from your butcher several days before needed. Have the butcher trim uncut pork ribs and form a crown, removing backbone for easy carving).
1/2 teaspoon rosemary leaves, crushed
1 teaspoon seasoned salt

Stuffing
1/2 pound of your favorite, seasoned sausage meat
2-3 stalks celery, thinly sliced
1/2 pound fresh mushrooms, sliced
1 large onion, chopped
1 tablespoon dried parsley
1/2 teaspoon salt
1/2 teaspoon white pepper
2 cups cooked rice (Uncle Ben's preferred)

Microwave crumbled sausage in a 2-quart casserole on HIGH for 2-3 minutes. Break up with fork and place on paper towel to drain. Place celery, mushrooms and onions in same dish that sausage was in and microwave for 5-6 minutes on HIGH. Stir in sausage along with remaining ingredients. Set aside while preparing roast for microwaving.

Insert meat thermometer (if used) in a meaty area between two ribs, making sure thermometer does not touch bone or fat. Place roast on microwave rack with bony ends down. Rub with rosemary leaves and seasoned salt until dissolved. Cook roast on HIGH for 5-8 minutes.

The following cycle of cooking will be at 50% power for 15-17 minutes per pound.

1. Halfway through the final cycle turn roast over with rib end up.
2. Insert meat thermometer (if used) in a meaty area between the ribs, making sure the thermometer does not touch bone or fat, and microwave until about 20 minutes of cooking time remains.
3. Fill roast cavity lightly with rice stuffing, covering **stuffing only** with plastic wrap to prevent drying out. Save remaining stuffing to place around roast when served.
4. Cook remaining time, or until the internal temperature reaches 165⁰F.
5. Remove from microwave and cover roast loosely with foil. Let stand 10-20 minutes, or until temperature reaches 170⁰F.

Transfer roast to serving platter, using a large metal spatula to support stuffing. Garnish rib end with spiced crab apples, pieces of orange or paper frills. To serve carve between chops.

For an attractive centerpiece or elegant buffet table, fashion ham to resemble a peacock. Score and stud the ham with cloves. Attach a carved sweet potato for the head, with a ruffle around the neck, olives for eyes, frilled party picks for a crown, and for the tail attach a fan of skewered fruits.

Ham Cookery

The secret to a tender, flavorful ham cooked in the microwave is *slow* cooking—yet cooking time will be half that of conventional cooking!

Kind of Ham	Approx. min./lb.	Start at HIGH POWER	Finish at 40% POWER
Picnic Shoulder (Cook-before-eating kind)	16-18	8 min.	160° F
Picnic Shoulder (Fully cooked)	16-18	5 min.	130° F
Bone-In (Cook-before-eating kind)	16-18	8 min.	160° F
Bone-in (Fully cooked)	12-14	5 min.	130° F
Canned Ham	6-8	4 min.	130° F
Boneless rolled ham	6-8	4 min.	130° F

Tips for Ham Cookery

Place ham on rack to cook. (If rack isn't available, use an inverted saucer on which to place ham.)

If a shield is used it should be at least 1 inch from the walls and 3 inches from the top of oven.

Remove from oven. Loosely tent with foil and allow to stand 10 minutes. Temperature will rise at least 5°F - 10°F.

Stir-Fry Beef or Pork

Have dinner in less than 15 minutes.
A good time to use a food processor!

Serves 4

1 pound ground beef or pork (veal may also be used)
3 tablespoons soy sauce (or to taste)
3 tablespoons sesame seed oil (this adds a special flavor)
8 cups shredded cabbage
2 carrots, sliced thinly (diagonally)
3-4 green onions, sliced thinly (use tops also)
2 garlic cloves
Dash of ginger

Microwave ground beef or pork 5-6 minutes on HIGH. Add 1 tablespoon each of soy sauce and sesame seed oil. Cover and set aside. Combine cabbage, onions, carrots, garlic, 2 additional tablespoons of soy sauce and sesame oil. Microwave covered 4-5 minutes until lightly steamed (cabbage should not be soft). Combine vegetables with meat and add a dash of ginger, salt, pepper, additional soy and sesame oil to taste. Delicious served with a fruit salad and a loaf of bread.

Ham and Broccoli Bundles with Pimento Cheese Sauce

Perfect for a luncheon dish.

4 thin slices of cooked ham
Prepared mustard
10-ounce package of frozen broccoli stalks
Pimento cheese sauce

Thaw frozen broccoli stalks 2-3 minutes on 30% power or defrost. Spread ham slices lightly with mustard. Wrap each slice around drained broccoli stalks. Place in greased baking dish. Brush with melted butter. Cover tightly and cook on HIGH 4-5 minutes. While broccoli stands, make pimento cheese sauce.

Pimento Cheese Sauce

3 tablespoons flour
3 tablespoons butter
1/4 teaspoon salt
1/4 teaspoon white pepper
1 cup milk
2 tablespoons diced pimentos
1 cup shredded cheese

Make white sauce by melting butter 45 seconds on HIGH. Add flour, salt and pepper and pimentos, stirring to blend. Add milk. Cook for 3-5 minutes on 70% power, stirring several times. After mixture thickens, add cheese, stirring until well blended. Serve hot over ham rolls.

Braised Barbecue Ribs
Ribs are so tender they almost slip from the bone.

Serves 4

4 pounds spareribs, cut in 2-3 inch pieces
1 1/4 cups barbecue sauce (see recipe below)
1 lemon, thinly sliced

Arrange ribs in bottom 12 x 8-inch dish or 3-quart casserole. Arrange lemon slices over top. Cover tightly with plastic wrap. Cook on HIGH 5 minutes. Reduce power to 40% and cook for 20-25 minutes. Drain. Turn ribs over and rearrange so least cooked ribs are to the outside. Overlap more cooked parts. Add barbecue sauce and re-cover tightly with plastic wrap. Microwave 20-25 minutes at 40% power until fork tender.

"Smoked" Barbecue Sauce
Delicious on pork ribs, meat balls and chicken.
Liquid Smoke is the secret.

Yields 2 cups

1/2 cup onions, finely chopped
2 garlic cloves, minced
2 cups ketchup
1/3 cup brown sugar
1/4 cup cider vinegar
1/2 cup water
1/4 cup Worcestershire sauce
Few drops Tabasco
1 tablespoon Liquid Smoke

Place onions and garlic in a 1-quart container. Cover with plastic wrap and cook for 2-3 minutes on HIGH. Add remaining ingredients and cook for 4 minutes on HIGH and 4-6 minutes on 50% power. Store leftover sauce in refrigerator and use on chicken, pork or beef.

Barbecued Spareribs

Precook ribs in the microwave and finish up on the grill, saving lots of time without sacrificing that wonderful barbecue flavor.

4 pounds lean spareribs, cut into individual ribs
Barbecue Sauce

Place ribs on side in large rectangular dish. Cover loosely with waxed paper and cook on HIGH 18-20 minutes until fork tender. (Rearrange ribs after cooking first 10 minutes). Drain and transfer to grill. Cook 10 minutes. Brush with sauce and cook 5 minutes, turning several times.

Ground Pork Patties
Speedy and Delicious with an Oriental flavor.
Use browning tray.

1 pound ground pork
2 small green onions, chopped
1 chopped tomato
3 eggs

Add onion, tomato and eggs to ground pork and form into patties. Preheat browning tray for 8-9 minutes. Cook on HIGH 2 minutes on first side and 2-3 minutes on second side. Add soy sauce to each patty and eat like a hamburger.

Lamb with Herb Mustard Coating
Microwaved Lamb gives juicy, tender results!

1/2 teaspoon rosemary
1 clove garlic, mashed
1 tablespoon soy sauce
1/2 cup Dijon mustard
1/4 cup olive oil or cooking oil
Leg of lamb (a small leg of lamb,
    or a larger more
    mature lamb shank half.)

Mix rosemary, garlic, soy and mustard in a small bowl. Using a wire whip, beat in oil a few droplets at a time to make an emulsion. This makes about 1 cup of coating.

Place the lamb on a rack in a baking dish, fat side down. If your oven permits the use of foil, shield the end of the leg bone with aluminum foil to cover about 2 inches of meat. This will prevent overcooking.

Spread half the coating on top of the lamb before cooking. If using a food sensor, insert it into the meat so that it is not touching fat or bone and the tip of the sensor is in the center of a large meat muscle. Microwave at 50% power to:

120°F for rare lamb
135°F for medium
150°F for well done

If you are **not** using a food sensor, but are cooking by time rather than temperature, allow about:

10 minutes per pound for rare
11 minutes per pound for medium
12 minutes per pound for well-done

Estimate total cooking time and turn the lamb over about halfway through cooking. Drain the fat from the dish and spread the remaining coating mixture on the lamb after turning.

Continue to drain the fat from the dish as it accumulates during cooking. Turn the dish during cooking, as required by your oven to give even cooking results. Some ovens require more turning than others. Serve with the coating.

Beef Burgundy

Yield 6 servings

1 1/2 pounds flank steak or sirloin
Freshly ground black pepper
3 garlic cloves, minced
2 tablespoons bacon drippings or butter
1 medium onion, thinly sliced
1/2 pound fresh mushrooms, sliced
1 cup sour cream
2 tablespoons flour
1 cup sharp Cheddar cheese, grated
1/2 cup Burgundy or red wine
1/4 teaspoon each: basil, marjoram, and thyme
2 teaspoons salt

Cut flank steak in very thin slices across the grain while meat is still partially frozen. Combine garlic cloves, onions, mushrooms, wine and seasonings and cook in a covered dish for 5 minutes on HIGH. Blend flour with sour cream and add to seasoning mixture and allow to cook for 5-8 additional minutes on 70% power. Set aside and cook flank steak in bacon drippings or oil on HIGH 3-4 minutes. Stir halfway through cooking. Add sauce mixture and cheese to beef and stir to blend. Cook 1-3 minutes longer on 70% power. Serve over noodles or rice. Garnish with sautéed mushroom slices and chopped fresh parsley.

Mrs. Stancil's Spaghetti Sauce

Serves 6

1 pound ground lean beef
1/2 pound Italian sausage
1 (1 pound, 13 ounce) can tomatoes
1 (6-ounce) can tomato paste
1 large, thinly sliced onion (or 1 package dry onion soup mix)
1 piece of pork, such as a ham bone or pork chop
2 teaspoons oregano
1/2 teaspoon marjoram
3 garlic cloves, minced
1 bay leaf
2 teaspoons salt
1 tablespoon sugar
1 teaspoon black pepper

Cook ground beef, Italian sausage and onions for 5-8 minutes on HIGH until no longer pink. Stir and drain. Add remaining ingredients and cook for 20 minutes on HIGH. Stir and microwave for 40-50 minutes on 50% power. Taste and adjust seasonings. Cook an additional 30 minutes if your prefer a long-simmered flavor.

If Italian sausage is not available sauté 1 tablespoon fennel seed in 2 tablespoons oil on HIGH for 1 minute. Let stand about 5 minutes for flavors to blend and then strain oil into spaghetti sauce. Add 1/2 pound ground pork or beef instead of sausage. Since fennel is used to flavor Italian sausage it will add this same flavor to the sauce.

Leg of Lamb with Potatoes
Serve with mint jelly.

5-7 pound leg of lamb (excess fat removed)
3-4 garlic cloves
1 tablespoon vegetable oil
1 tablespoon bottled browning sauce
1/2 teaspoon freshly ground pepper
1 pound "new" potatoes

Make slits over entire surface of lamb every three inches and insert small pieces of garlic in slits. Rub lamb with combined vegetable oil and browning sauce. Sprinkle with pepper. Place lamb with thick side down on roasting rack. Cover loosely with waxed paper. Cook at 50% power for 10 minutes per pound for rare, or 11 minutes per pound for medium. Turn meat over halfway through cooking (unless your oven requires more turning.) While roast is standing, place potatoes in drippings from roast and cook on HIGH for 5-8 minutes.

If using temperature probe, insert in thickest portion of meat without touching bone. Cook to 145°F. for medium-rare, and 160°F. for medium to well-done lamb.

Spaghetti Pie

6-8 servings

Crust:
8 ounces spaghetti, cooked
1/3 cup Parmesan cheese
1 tablespoon butter
1 egg, beaten

Filling:
1/2 pound ground beef
1/2 pound sausage
1/2 cup onion
2-3 garlic cloves, minced
1 (15-ounce) can tomato sauce
1 tablespoon sugar
1/2 teaspoon salt
1/2 teaspoon pepper
1 teaspoon basil
1 teaspoon oregano
1 cup cottage cheese
1/2 cup Mozzarella cheese

Mix spaghetti, Parmesan cheese, eggs and butter in large bowl. Turn onto large platter, pressing spaghetti evenly to bottom and sides to form a crust. Cook on HIGH 3-5 minutes. Place beef, sausage, onions and garlic in 2-quart bowl and cook on HIGH for 5-7 minutes. Stir occasionally. Drain off fat. Add tomato sauce and all seasonings. Cook 6-8 minutes on HIGH. Spread cottage cheese over spaghetti crust. Pour tomato and meat mixture over cottage cheese. Cover tightly with plastic wrap and cook on HIGH 6-8 minutes until heated thoroughly. Add Mozzarella and serve at once.

Pizza Crust

Yield: 2 12 inch crusts

1 cup warm water (105°F - 115°F)
1 package active dry yeast
2 tablespoons shortening
1/2 teaspoon salt
4 cups all-purpose flour
1 tablespoon salad oil

Place warm water and yeast in mixing bowl or food processor. Add shortening, salt and half the flour. Mix well until smooth. Gradually add remaining flour until stiff dough is formed. Knead by hand 8-10 minutes, or process for 30 seconds, using sharp blade of your food processor. Check, and if dough is not smooth and elastic, continue to process in 15 second bursts until the desired consistency is reached. Place in greased bowl and cover with plastic wrap. Speed-rise if desired by microwaving for 6 minutes on 10% power and allowing to stand 10 minutes before repeating process. When double in size (60 minutes if not speed rising), punch down and divide in half. Roll out and place on greased 12-inch pizza pan. Add pizza sauce, along with your favorite fillings, such as Mozzarella cheese, anchovies, sausage, green pepper, onion, mushrooms, etc. Cook conventionally for 20-25 minutes in a preheated 450°F oven.

Papa Joe's Pizza Filling

Yield: 4 servings
Makes 2 2/3 cups filling, enough for two 12-inch pizzas

1 tablespoon salad oil
1/2 cup chopped onion
4 garlic cloves, minced
1 (1 pound-3 ounces) can whole tomatoes
1 (8-ounce) can tomato sauce
1 bay leaf
1 teaspoon each salt, oregano and basil
1 tablespoon sugar
Add pepper to taste
Add meat and other toppings to taste

Microwave onion and garlic cloves in oil for 2-3 minutes on HIGH. Add remaining ingredients and microwave 15 minutes on HIGH. Reduce to 50% power for 10 minutes. (Simmering helps develop good flavor.)

Pork Chop Casserole

4 pork chops (3/4-inch thick)
2-3 medium sized potatoes, sliced thinly
1 medium onion, sliced thinly
1/4 teaspoon basil and oregano
1 (10 1/2-ounce) can Cheddar cheese soup
1/4 cup milk
1/2 cup Parmesan cheese
Salt and pepper to taste

Place chops in bottom of baking dish. Layer potatoes and onions on top of chops. Mix cheese soup with Parmesan cheese, milk and spices. Pour over chops. Cover with plastic wrap and cook at 70% power for 20-25 minutes. Rearrange midway through cooking time.

Meat Loaf

5-6 servings

1 1/2 pounds lean ground beef
2 eggs, well beaten
1 medium onion, chopped
2 stalks celery, thinly sliced
1/3 cup green pepper, chopped
2 carrots, finely grated
1 tablespoon horseradish
1 teaspoon dry mustard
1 tablespoon parsley
1 teaspoon garlic salt
1/2 teaspoon pepper
1/3 cup ketchup

Toss all ingredients (except ketchup) gently with two forks. Cook in a 10-inch round baking dish with an inverted custard cup in center. (A bundt cake pan may also be used.) Place meat mixture in a ring around the custard cup. Cook for 5 minutes on HIGH and 10-15 minutes on 50% power. During last several minutes add ketchup. Allow to stand 5 minutes before serving.

🔥 If you would like to serve the meat loaf ring on another plate or platter, after 5 minutes standing time cover with plate or platter and invert the ring and custard cup. The custard cup should hold excess grease if the vacuum was not disturbed during resting time. Add additional ketchup and garnish with herbs and parsley.

Mongolian Beef

Serves 4

1 pound sliced flank steak
2 cups shredded scallions
8-10 cloves garlic, finely minced
2 tablespoons oil
2 teaspoons sesame oil
1/2 teaspoon salt

Marinade:

4 tablespoons soy sauce
1 tablespoon dry sherry
1 teaspoon black pepper
3 tablespoons cold water
2 tablespoons cornstarch
1 teaspoon sugar
1 tablespoon oil

Slice the flank steak in very thin slices across the grain while meat is partially frozen. Combine marinade ingredients in a bowl, add sliced beef, mix thoroughly and set aside for at least 30 minutes. Meat-marinade combination may be refrigerated overnight or frozen for later use. Microwave the oil, garlic and beef, covered, about 3 minutes on HIGH. Stir in 2 tablespoons soy sauce. Microwave scallions, covered, 1 minute and stir in meat. Microwave 1 minute longer, add 2 teaspoons sesame oil. Serve with noodles.

Marinated Barbequed Pork Chops

Yield: 4 servings

1/2 cup vegetable oil
1/4 cup olive oil
1/4 cup lemon juice
3 cloves garlic, crushed
1 teaspoon salt
1 teaspoon paprika
1/2 teaspoon pepper
6 bay leaves
2 tablespoons Liquid Smoke
4 (1-inch thick) loin or rib pork chops

Combine first 8 ingredients in a shallow baking dish and mix well. Add meat to marinade; cover and marinate over-night in refrigerator. Preheat browning grill 8 or 9 minutes (or as manufacturer directs) and cook 5 minutes on first side and 5-6 minutes on second side.

Beef Flank Steak
With
Dr. Jim's Special Marinade Sauce

Marinate steak first for 4-6 hours in Dr. Jim's Special Marinade Sauce and then cook on the browning grill.

1 1/2 pounds beef flank steak
1 1/2 cups salad oil
1/4 cup Worcestershire sauce
1/4 teaspoon salt
1/2 cup vinegar
2 teaspoons garlic salt
3/4 cup soy sauce
2 tablespoons mustard
1 tablespoon black pepper
1 1/2 teaspoon parsley flakes
1/3 cup lemon juice

Place all of above ingredients, except steak, into a blender. Blend until contents are thoroughly mixed (about 30 seconds). Mix in a shaker if a blender is not available. Place steak in a glass container and pour marinade over it. Cover container and place in the refrigerator for 4-6 hours. This marinade may be refrigerated and used over again.

Preheat browning grill or skillet for 8-9 minutes on HIGH or according to manufacturer's instructions. While grill is preheating drain steak and blot with paper towel. Add 2 pats of butter to preheated grill and microwave for 3 minutes on first side and 2-3 minutes on second side for a medium rare steak.

🐷 This marinade may be stored in the refrigerator for up to 2 months. However, after beef roast or steak has been marinated in it, do not refrigerate and use for any longer than 3 weeks.

Taglarina
A good dish to prepare ahead and freeze!

Serves 12-15

2 pounds lean ground beef
1 cup onion, chopped
4 cloves garlic, minced
1 bell pepper, chopped
1 tablespoon chili powder
1 teaspoon basil
1/2 teaspoon oregano
1 tablespoon Worcestershire sauce
1 tablespoon sugar
1 1/2 teaspoons salt
1/2 teaspoon pepper
1 (16-ounce) can tomatoes
1 (16-ounce) can shoe peg corn, drained
1 (8-ounce) can tomato sauce
1 (4-ounce) can ripe olives, sliced and olive juice
6-8 ounces spaghetti, cooked
2 cups Cheddar cheese, shredded

Place ground beef, onion, garlic and bell pepper in a 2-quart glass measure and cook for 10-12 minutes on HIGH. Drain and add seasonings, tomatoes, corn and tomato sauce. Add olives and olive juice. Taste to adjust seasonings. Add spaghetti, stirring to blend. Pour into 2 casserole dishes. (This is better if flavors are allowed to blend overnight in the refrigerator.) Cook each dish for 10-12 minutes at 70% power or until hot.

Stuffed Green Peppers

4 servings

4 large green peppers
1 pound lean ground beef
1 medium onion, peeled and chopped
1/4 cup chopped celery
1 1/2 cups long-grained rice, cooked
1 (16-ounce) can tomato sauce
2 garlic cloves, minced
1 teaspoon salt
1/2 teaspoon basil
Freshly ground black pepper

Prepare peppers by cutting a thin slice from the stem end. Remove seeds with a teaspoon. Combine beef and onions in a glass casserole and cook for 3-5 minutes on HIGH. Combine ground beef and onions with remaining ingredients, mixing well. Stuff peppers with mixture and place on baking dish, covering tightly with plastic wrap. Microwave 12-16 minutes on 70% power.

Boneless meats cook more evenly than meats with a bone because the bone attracts microwave energy.

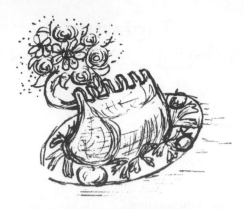

Standing Rib Roast
Could be a Father's Day speciality!

Serves 4-6

4 pound beef standing rib roast

Place roast fat side down on a rack or inverted saucer placed in a baking dish. (Shield tail of roast if roast weighs over 5 pounds.) Make sure roast always stays out of juices, because this will produce a steamed or pot-roasted flavor. Estimate total cooking time following chart below:

Desired Doneness	Min./lb.	Removal Temperature
Rare	9-12	120°F
Medium	10-14	135°F
Well Done	11-15	150°F

Figure total cooking time and divide in half. Microwave on HIGH for 7-8 minutes. Microwave remainder of first half at 50% power. Turn roast with fat side up and insert microwave thermometer if desired. Cook at 50% power until temperature reaches desired level. Remove from oven, cover with foil and allow to stand 10-20 minutes before serving.

Ten-Minute Beef Stroganoff

Serves 4-5

1 pound round steak
1 (3-ounce) can mushroom slices with liquid
**   (or 2/3 cup fresh mushrooms sautéed in 2 tablespoons butter)**
1 envelope dry onion soup mix
1 cup dairy sour cream
2 tablespoons catsup
1/4 teaspoon garlic powder
3 tablespoons butter
2 tablespoons flour

Trim fat from meat. Cut meat diagonally across the grain in very thin strips. (It is easier to cut thinly if meat is slightly frozen first). Melt butter for 45-60 seconds on HIGH. Add meat and cook for 3 minutes on HIGH. Add 2/3 cup water and mushrooms. Stir in soup mix and heat to boiling. Mix sour cream with flour, stirring to blend. Add hot mixture. Add catsup and garlic powder. Cook on 70% power until mixture thickens. Do not overcook or meat will be tough. Serve over rice or noodles.

Sausage and Wild Rice Casserole

Yield 5-6 servings

1 package (6-ounce) long grain and wild rice, cooked
1 pound bulk sausage
1 cup chopped green onions, including stems
1 (10 3/4-ounce) can chicken broth
1/2 pound fresh mushrooms or
    2 (3-ounce) cans
1/4 cup half-and-half cream
2 tablespoons flour
1/2 tablespoons monosodium glutamate

Place crumbled sausage into a 2-quart casserole. Microwave on HIGH 5-6 minutes until done. (Do not overcook). Drain on paper towel and remove all but 2 tablespoons of fat from casserole. Sauté onions and mushrooms for 3-4 minutes on HIGH. Add flour and stir to blend. Add cream and chicken broth. Cook for 4-5 minutes until thickened. Add seasonings and combine all ingredients. Pour into casserole and microwave on 70% power for 10-15 minutes.

Liver and Onions

4-5 servings

4-6 slices bacon cut in thirds
1/4 cup flour
1 1/2 teaspoons salt
1 teaspoon black pepper
1 pound liver (sliced into serving size pieces)
2 cups onions, thinly sliced
1/2 cup water

Microwave bacon in a 12 x 8-inch dish on HIGH for 4-6 minutes. While bacon cooks, combine flour with salt and pepper. Dredge liver in flour, sprinkling excess flour over pieces. Set aside. Remove all but 2 tablespoons bacon fat and place liver in dish. Add onions and water, saving bacon to be crumbled over liver at end of cooking time. Cover with plastic wrap and microwave on HIGH 5 minutes. Reduce power to 50% and microwave 10-15 minutes until fork tender. Turn liver over and rearrange after first half of cooking time.

Quick Barbecue Burger

Yield: 8 servings

1 pound ground beef
1/2 cup onion
1/4 cup celery, finely chopped
1/4 cup green pepper
1/2 teaspoon garlic salt
1/4 teaspoon pepper
1/2 to 2/3 cup barbecue sauce
8 hamburger buns, toasted

Place ground beef, onion, celery and green pepper in a 2-quart casserole and microwave on HIGH for 5-8 minutes, stirring occasionally. Add remaining ingredients and cook on 50% power covered for 4-5 minutes. Spoon over buns and serve immediately.

Italian Style Sloppy Joes

6 servings

1 pound ground beef
1/2 cup chopped onion
1 can (8-ounce) tomato sauce
1/4 cup Parmesan cheese
1/2 cup grated sharp Cheddar cheese
1/4 teaspoon oregano
1/8 teaspoon basil
1/4 teaspoon garlic powder
Salt and pepper to taste
6 hamburger buns
6 slices Mozzarella cheese

Crumble ground beef in a 1-quart casserole and microwave on HIGH 5-7 minutes. Stir occasionally to break up meat; drain. Add remaining ingredients, except buns and Mozzarella cheese. Cook on HIGH 2-3 minutes until mixture starts to simmer. Microwave on 50% power for 4-6 minutes, stirring once. Spoon mixture on bottom half of bun and top with slice of Mozzarella cheese and bun top. Serve at once.

Onion Mushroom Sauce
Delicious served with Grilled Steak!

1 pound fresh mushrooms, sliced
1 cup thinly sliced onions
1/4 cup butter
1/2 cup white wine
3 tablespoons Worcestershire sauce
3 tablespoons soy sauce
1/2 teaspoon oregano
1/4 teaspoon garlic salt
1/4 teaspoon rosemary
1 tablespoon fresh parsley

Microwave mushrooms for 2-3 minutes on HIGH. Drain and add remaining ingredients cooking for 5-6 minutes on 30% power. Spoon over steak or serve as a side dish.

To remove stains and brown spots from browning skillet or dish, use baking soda for a speedy cleanup.

Use the microwave as a big time saver by combination cooking. Microwave meats first in the microwave—finishing up on the outdoor grill or smoker!

Marinate less tender cuts of meat for several hours, or overnight. Add slightly less liquid than if cooking conventionally and cover tightly with plastic wrap. Slower cooking tenderizes meat. Use a setting of 50% power or below.

Simply Scrumptious
Clay Pot Cookery

Clay Pot Cookery

General Guidelines

The use of the clay pot in the microwave is a combination of two excellent cooking methods. The clay pot is one of the oldest cooking utensils and the microwave is one of the fastest methods of cooking.

The clay pot is porous and should be soaked before each use. The clay pot then slowly releases the water during the cooking process. Less tender cuts of meat become tender, dried beans become a gourmet delight, and specialty dishes become simple and delicious.

The clay pot instruction book should be followed concerning soaking times. The first time the cooker is used the soaking time is longer.

Be sure the clay pot you are using is suitable for use in the microwave. Try the one minute test by placing an empty clay cooker in the microwave for one minute on HIGH. If the clay pot is hot to the touch at the end of the minute time period, the pot is not designed for use in the microwave. Many manufacturers recommend placing a cup of water in the oven when testing the micro-safety of a dish. Some microwave ovens can be operated for a short period of time empty. Check the use and care manual.

A general rule of thumb for cooking meat items is 5 minutes per pound on HIGH and 15 minutes per pound on 50% power. Food should stand covered at least 5 minutes before serving.

The basic principles of microwave cookery should also be followed when cooking with a clay pot.

Cornish Hens with Wild Rice
An elegant dish that will win raves!

1 (6-ounce) box Uncle Ben's long grain and wild rice
1 cup water
1/2 pound mushrooms (sliced)
1 (10-ounce) can condensed golden mushroom soup
2 Cornish hens (weight to total 2 to 2 1/2 pounds)
Salt Cornish hens to taste

Combine all ingredients except Cornish hens in water-soaked clay pot. Stir thoroughly. Place Cornish hens on top of mixture. Salt hens to taste. Cover with water-soaked lid and microwave 15 minutes on HIGH. Turn Cornish hens over and stir rice mixture -- especially around the outside edges of clay pot. Microwave for 30 to 35 minutes on 50% power, or until rice and hens are done. Let stand 5 minutes.

Chicken or Turkey Stock

2 pounds chicken necks, backs, and wings (or turkey parts)
3 stalks celery
3 carrots, washed but not scraped
1 medium onion
6 peppercorns (or 1 teaspoon black pepper)
1 1/2 teaspoons salt

Combine all ingredients in water-soaked clay pot. Fill with water within 2 inches of top. Cover and microwave in water-soaked clay pot for 15 minutes on HIGH and then reduce to 50% power for 45 minutes, or until done.

Barbecued Pork Ribs
Quick, Easy, and Delicious!

3 pounds pork ribs (small meaty ribs should be used)

Sauce:
1/2 cup bottled barbecue sauce
1/4 cup Italian dressing
1 teaspoon dried parsley flakes
1 medium onion, finely chopped

Place ribs in water-soaked clay pot. Cook for 15 minutes on HIGH. Drain off all liquid. Cover ribs in barbecue sauce. Cook for 25 minutes on 50% power. Turn ribs and baste with barbecue sauce. Cook 20 minutes more on 50% power.

If ribs are prepared ahead of time: Slice into individual ribs and place in glass casserole dish. Baste ribs with barbecue sauce. Reheat for 5 to 10 minutes on 80% power, serve, eat, and enjoy!

New England Boiled Dinner
This is excellent served with rye bread and mustard.

serves 4 to 6

2 1/2 to 3 pounds corned beef brisket with
   seasonings
3 small onions, sliced
1 small head of cabbage, cut in wedges
6 small potatoes
6 carrots
Parsley to garnish

Place corned beef, seasonings, and onion in water-soaked clay pot. Cover with water-soaked lid. Microwave on 50% power for 30 minutes. Turn corned beef and add cabbage, potatoes, carrots and onions and re-cover. Continue cooking 70 to 75 minutes on 50% power or until meat is tender. Let stand 5 minutes before serving. Sprinkle parsley over corned beef and vegetables. (This meal takes 4 to 5 hours to cook conventionally.)

Beans a la Delicious
A plain bean is turned into a gourmet delight!

1 pound dried beans (Pinto or
  Great Northern Beans)
5 cups water
1 large onion, chopped
1 garlic clove, minced
1 teaspoon salt
1/8 teaspoon white pepper
1 ham bone

Rinse beans and place in a deep dish. Cover with two inches of water. Microwave on HIGH until water comes to a boil and boils rapidly for 2 minutes. Let stand for 1 hour or more. Drain water into measuring cup and add enough for 5 cups of water.

Place all ingredients in water-soaked clay pot. Stir well. Cover with water-soaked clay lid. Microwave 15 minutes on HIGH. Stir and cover. Microwave for 30 to 35 minutes on 50% power. Stir and cover. Continue to cook on 50% power for 60 to 65 minutes or until beans are tender. Let stand 10 minutes.

Mezetti
An all-time favorite! Try it and be prepared to have many
more requests for this dish.

Serves 6 to 8

1 pound ground beef
1 medium onion, finely chopped
1/4 cup green pepper, chopped
1/4 cup celery, chopped
1 (8-ounce) package fine egg noodles
2 garlic cloves, minced
1 to 3 teaspoons chili powder (season to taste)
1/2 teaspoon paprika
1 teaspoon salt
1 (10-ounce) can tomato soup
1 (10-ounce) can mushroom soup
1 (4-ounce) can mushroom pieces, drained
1 cup water
3/4 cup cheddar cheese, shredded

Place ground beef, green pepper, onion, celery, and garlic in water-soaked clay pot. Cover with water-soaked lid. Cook on HIGH for 6 minutes. Drain off excess liquid. Sprinkle noodles on meat mixture. Stir together in a bowl, chili powder, paprika, salt, tomato soup, mushroom soup, mushrooms, and water. Pour mixture over meat and noodles. Re-cover and microwave on HIGH for 10 minutes and on 50% power for 15 to 18 minutes or until noodles are cooked. Sprinkle cheese on top and cover. Let stand 5 minutes.

Deirdre's Chicken Dinner

1 2 to 3 pound fryer
1 (6-ounce) box Quick-cooking long grain and and wild rice·
1 1/2 cups water
1 medium onion, chopped
1 stalk celery, chopped

Stuff chicken cavity with onion and celery. Place chicken in water-soaked clay pot breast side down. Cover with water-soaked lid. Microwave on HIGH for 10 minutes. Remove chicken. Add wild rice mix and water to cooker and stir to blend. Place chicken breast side up and cook 30 to 45 minutes on 70% power, or until chicken is tender. Let stand covered 5 minutes.

Pork Chops and Sauerkraut Dinner

serves 4 to 6

4 to 6 pork chops (approximately 2 pounds)
2 onions sliced in rings
1 (27-ounce) can sauerkraut, well drained and rinsed
2 large potatoes, sliced
2 large apples, sliced
1/2 cup white wine
2 teaspoons instant chicken bouillon
1 teaspoon caraway seeds (optional)
1 tablespoon parsley flakes
1/2 teaspoon cracked pepper or black pepper
4 ounces salt pork, finely diced

Place all ingredients in water-soaked clay pot. Stir well. Place pork chops on top of mixture. Cover with water-soaked lid. Cook for 15 minutes on HIGH. Turn pork chops and stir mixture gently. Cook 45 to 55 minutes on 50% power or until pork chops are tender. Let stand 5 minutes before serving.

Southern Style Green Beans
Tastes like Grandmother's!

2 cups water
3 slices bacon, cut in small pieces
1 medium onion, chopped
1 teaspoon instant beef bouillon
1 tablespoon bacon drippings
1 teaspoon salt
1 1/2 to 2 pounds green beans, cut in half and trimmed

Combine water, bacon, onion and bouillon in water-soaked clay cooker. Microwave on HIGH 5 to 7 minutes until water is very hot. Add beans, salt and bacon drippings to hot water. Cover with water-soaked lid. Microwave on HIGH 5 minutes. Stir and re-cover. Cook on 50% power 40 to 50 minutes. Let stand covered 5 minutes.

Porcupines
Children especially love this!

serves 4 to 6

1 pound ground beef
1 medium onion, chopped
1/4 teaspoon celery seeds
1/2 teaspoon salt
1/2 teaspoon garlic salt
1/8 teaspoon pepper
1/3 cup uncooked rice
1/4 cup green pepper, chopped
1 teaspoon Worcestershire sauce
1 (10-ounce) can tomato soup
1/4 cup water

Mix all ingredients except tomato soup and water in mixing bowl. Shape into meatballs (about 1 1/2-inch diameter). Put meatballs in water-soaked pot and cover with water-soaked lid. Microwave on HIGH for 5 minutes. Drain liquid. Mix tomato soup and water and pour over meatballs. Re-cover and miorowave for 30 to 35 minutes on 50% power, or until meatballs are done. Let stand 5 minutes.

Nicole's Chili
Great with crackers and dill pickles.

serves 6 to 8

1 pound ground beef
1 large onion, chopped
1/2 green pepper, chopped
1 cup celery, chopped (optional)
2 garlic cloves, minced
1 (16-ounce) can tomatoes, mashed
1 (8-ounce) can tomato sauce
1 to 3 tablespoons chili powder
1 can (12-ounces) V-8 Juice
1 cup water
1 teaspoon basil
1 teaspoon salt
1 tablespoon paprika
2 (1-pound) can beans drained (chili, kidney or pinto)

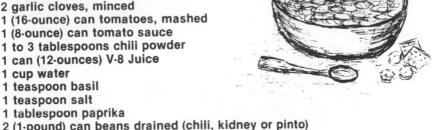

Place ground beef, onion, pepper, celery, and garlic in water-soaked clay pot. Cover and microwave on HIGH for 7 to 10 minutes. Drain off excess liquid. Add remaining ingredients, except beans. Re-cover and cook 30 minutes on 50% power. Add beans and stir well. Continue to cook 10 minutes on 50% power. Let stand covered 5 minutes.

If arcing occurs in your oven, turn oven off immediately; this can cause damage to the oven interior surface or cooking utensil. Arcing is an electrical current which flows from the wall of the oven to a metal object in the oven, causing a light flash and popping sound. Improper metal usage causes the problem.

Christy's Beef Stew

Especially good with cornbread!

1 1/2 pounds beef stew meat, cubed
3 medium potatoes, cubed
3 carrots, sliced
1 large onion, chopped
1 garlic clove, minced
1 (8-ounce) can tomato sauce
1 cup water
1 teaspoon Worcestershire sauce
1 teaspoon salt
1/4 teaspoon pepper

Place all ingredients in a water-soaked clay pot. Stir and cover with water-soaked lid. Cook on HIGH for 15 minutes. Stir and re-cover. Microwave on 50% power 45 to 50 minutes, or until meat and potatoes are tender. Let stand covered 5 minutes.

Simply Scrumptious
Breads

Breads

General Guidelines

You will find that the microwave can be an asset when baking bread, saving time and energy. You may use it most effectively by combining microwave and conventional cooking. Some of the recipes in this section are designed especially for complimentary cooking, taking the best from both worlds.

Listed below are tips to aid in successful bread making:

If your oven has an uneven cooking pattern, when proofing or baking bread, place the bread dish on an inverted saucer to give more even cooking results.

If your microwave has a probe, use it when heating milk or water so the yeast will work most effectively.

For most microwave baking use medium power or a 50% setting.

Grease dishes lightly and sprinkle with crumbs. The crumbs absorb excess moisture which forms between the bread and the dish during microwaving.

Do not overcook. Overcooked breads are tough.

To speed rise, use the following as a guide:

10% power - Microwave 10 to 12 minutes and allow to rest 15 minutes. Repeat if necessary. (Use this power level if your microwave has an uneven cooking pattern.)

30% power - Microwave 1 to 2 minutes and allow to stand 15 minutes.

50% power - Microwave 1 minute and let stand for 15 minutes. Repeat if necessary.

Croutons

4 cups cubed bread
1 tablespoon garlic herb seasoning

Place bread cubes in a round dish such as a pie plate. Sprinkle with seasoning. Cook on HIGH for 6-8 minutes, stirring every two minutes.

Magic Buttermilk Muffins
Tasty as a quick breakfast bread.

Yield 3 dozen

1 cup 100% Bran Cereal
1 cup boiling water
1/2 cup butter
1/2 cup oil
1 1/2 cups sugar
2 eggs
2 1/2 cups sifted all-purpose flour
2 1/2 teaspoons soda
1 teaspoon salt
2 cups All-Bran cereal
2 cups buttermilk
1 cup raisins or chopped dates

Boil water in glass cup in microwave. Pour over 100% Bran and allow to cool. Set aside. Cream butter, oil and sugar. Add eggs, one at a time, beating well after each addition. Add flour, soda, salt and buttermilk, mixing well. Add cereal, raisins, and nuts. Stir only until well mixed. Place cupcake liners in custard cups or in micro-safe muffin pan. Fill half-full with batter and cook 2 1/2 - 3 minutes on HIGH. Cover with plastic when removing from oven and allow to stand several minutes. This mixture will keep in a covered container up to 5 or 6 weeks in the refrigerator. Just dip mixture out as needed; do not stir.

Quick Butter Biscuits
This is a great recipe to use conventionally also. These biscuits are very good warmed in the microwave.

Yield 12 2-inch biscuits

1 stick butter (firm)
2 cups self-rising flour
2/3 cup cold milk

Cut butter into flour and add milk. Knead several times. Roll out and cut into biscuits. Preheat browning tray 6 minutes. Place biscuits in circle and cook for 1 minute on HIGH. Turn over and cook 1 - 1 1/2 minutes on HIGH.

Herbed Bread Sticks

1/2 cup butter, softened
1/2 teaspoon each of chives, tarragon, marjoram, parsley, garlic salt
2 tablespoons sesame seeds
3/4 loaf very thin bread (Pepperidge Farm)

Soften butter for 30 seconds on 50% power. Add spices and sesame seed. Spread on bread. Cut each piece of bread into 4 slices and microwave for 5-8 minutes stirring every two minutes. Enjoy with salads and soups.

Potato Rolls

These rolls could be called "never fail" and work very nicely using combination microwave and conventional cookery. Good to microwave to brown-and-serve stage, then freeze and cook conventionally later -- and still have that fresh yeast bread taste!

Yield 2 1/2 to 3 dozen

1 cup milk
2 tablespoons honey or molasses
1 tablespoon salt
1/3 cup butter, melted
1 cup warm water (105°F - 115°F.)
1 package active dry yeast
2 eggs
1 medium potato (or 1 cup mashed potatoes)
1 cup Miller's Bran (or raw unprocessed whole wheat flour)
4 1/2 - 5 1/2 cups all-purpose bread flour

Bake potato: Microwave pricked, well-scrubbed potato 4-5 minutes on HIGH and wrap in foil to stand several minutes. Peel and mash.

Prepare dough: Dissolve yeast in warm water. Combine milk, honey, salt, butter and well beaten eggs. Add mashed potato. Then add yeast-water mixture, Miller's bran and 2 cups of flour. Beat well for several minutes. Stir in enough flour to produce a slightly stiff dough. Turn dough out onto a lightly floured pastry cloth or board and knead until smooth and elastic, 8-10 minutes. Add only enough flour to keep dough from sticking to board or cloth. (On rainy days more flour will be required to keep from sticking.) Place dough in bowl that has been oiled with 2-3 tablespoons of cooking oil. Turn dough over once so that all sides are greased. Cover with plastic wrap and allow to rise until double in bulk, about 1 hour.

If you would like to speed up the rising process, place bread in glass or microwave-safe bowl in microwave and warm for 10-12 minutes on 10% power. Let stand for 10 minutes and repeat process if desired.

Microwave Cookery
Punch dough down and turn out onto kitchen counter and form a smooth ball. Pinch dough into 36 small balls, placing onto three well greased 9-inch pie plates. Cover tightly with plastic wrap and allow to rise until double in bulk. (Use speed rise process if desired). Cook each for 5-6 minutes on 50% power until set. At this point cool and freeze, to be enjoyed later by heating or browning conventionally. (You may also like to enjoy eating at once by placing under the broiler for 3-5 minutes).

Conventionally
Punch dough down and make out into rolls. Cover and let rise until double in bulk -- about 45 minutes. Bake at 400°F. for 15-20 minutes. This recipe works well as a refrigerator-type roll. Make dough and place in refrigerator. Make out into rolls the next day, following the same procedure for rising process.

For proofing or baking, placing the bread dish on an inverted saucer may give more even cooking results.

How to Defrost Frozen Yeast Bread Dough

Microwave 1 1/2 cups of water until boiling in a baking dish such as 12 x 8 inch.

Heavily grease an 8 x 4 x 5-inch loaf dish. Cut a piece of wax paper to fit and place in loaf dish. Grease the top of the paper. Butter frozen dough on all sides and place in loaf dish.

Put loaf dish in the 12 x 8-inch baking dish with the hot water.

Cover with wax paper and microwave for 2 minutes on 50% power. Turn dough over and microwave for 2 additional minutes.

Allow to stand 2 minutes. Dough should be defrosted and slightly warm. If not, microwave 1 minute at a time, turning dough over each time until thawed.

Corn Bread - Southern Style
Especially delicious with fresh vegetables!

4-5 servings

1 cup self-rising corn meal
2/3 cup buttermilk
1 egg
3 tablespoons cooking oil (or bacon drippings)

Mix ingredients (saving 1 tablespoon oil for browning dish), then preheat browning dish for 6 minutes. *(The secret to this recipe is allowing the mixture to stand at least 6 minutes before cooking - so the meal can absorb moisture.)* When browning dish or skillet is preheated, add remaining tablespoon of oil, and pour cornbread mix in. Cook for 3 minutes on HIGH. Turn over and cook for 1-2 additional minutes on HIGH.

If browning skillet or dish it not available, follow above recipe, adding 1 tablespoon oil to a round 9-inch dish and use the same cooking directions omitting turning over.

Southern Hoe Cake

2-3 servings

2/3 cup self-rising cornmeal
1/4 cup self-rising flour
1/2 cup water
**2 tablespoons cooking oil (save one tablespoon to add to skillet
    after preheating)**

Prepare hoe cake at least 5 minutes before preheating skillet so cornmeal will have time to absorb moisture before cooking. Blend ingredients together. Preheat browning skillet 6 minutes. Pour batter into dish and add 1 tablespoon oil. Cook on HIGH for 2 minutes on first side. Turn and cook 1-2 minutes longer.

Bonanza Bread
Nutritious and delicious.
Great for breakfast with cream cheese.

Yield 2 loaves

1 cup sifted all-purpose flour
1 cup whole wheat flour
1/2 teaspoon salt
1/2 teaspoon baking soda
1 1/2 teaspoons baking powder
2/3 cup nonfat dry milk
1/3 cup wheat germ
1/2 cup firmly packed brown sugar
3/4 cup mixed nuts (pecans, peanuts, walnuts, etc.)
1/2 cup raisins or dates
3 eggs
1/2 cup vegetable oil
1/2 cup molasses
2/3 cup orange juice
2 medium-size bananas, mashed
1/3 cup chopped dried apricots

Mix flour, salt, soda, baking powder, dry milk, wheat germ, sugar, nuts and raisins thoroughly with fork. Use food processor or blender to mix eggs, oil, molasses, orange juice and bananas; add apricots and process to chop coarsely. Combine two mixtures together and stir just until all flour is moistened and blended. Prepare two standard loaf dishes, by greasing well and placing wax paper on bottom of dish. Cook each loaf separately for 9 minutes at 50% power and for 3-5 minutes on HIGH. Cover with plastic wrap when removing from oven so moisture won't be lost. When cool, wrap tightly and store overnight, allowing flavors to mellow.

Sticky Buns
A speedy bread for breakfast in a hurry!

Yield 10 buns

1/4 cup butter
1/2 cup dark brown sugar
1/2 cup chopped nuts
1 (10-ounce) can refrigerated biscuits

Combine butter, sugar and nuts. Microwave for 1 1/2 minutes on HIGH in a 9-inch glass pie plate. Stir to blend. Separate biscuits and place in sugar mixture turning to coat both sides. Place a custard cup or glass in the center of the plate and arrange biscuits around edge. Microwave for 5-6 minutes on 70% power until biscuits are no longer doughy. Allow to stand several minutes before inverting onto plate.

Green Onion Batter Bread
Very moist the next day, too!

Yield 1 loaf

1/3 cup green onions, chopped (stems included)
1/2 cup grated Parmesan cheese
2 1/4 to 2 1/2 cups all-purpose flour
1/2 cup Miller's Bran (optional)
1 package active dry yeast
3/4 cup cream-style cottage cheese
1 teaspoon salt
1/2 cup water
2 tablespoons butter
1 egg
1/2 cup chopped fresh mushrooms (optional)

Place in large mixing bowl 1 1/4 cups flour, yeast, and green onion. Heat cottage cheese, water and butter until warm (115° - 120°F). Use probe or check temperature with candy thermometer. Combine with flour, salt, yeast and green onion, beating until smooth. Add remaining 1 cup of flour, Miller's Bran and egg. Beat until dough comes off beater in sheets. Pour batter into microwave-safe bowl to which 2 tablespoons of cooking oil have been added.' Cover tightly with plastic wrap.

Speed rise if desired by placing dough in microwave and warming at 10% power for 10-12 minutes and allowing to stand for 15 minutes. Repeat if necessary, until bread doubles in volume. Stir down and place in a greased 1 1/2-quart loaf dish or a microwave-safe ring mold that has been lined with well-greased waxed paper. Cover tightly and let rise until double in volume (about 45 minutes conventionally). Microwave proofing as described above may also be used.

Microwave for 7-9 minutes on 50% power. Cook until no longer doughy in center. If desired, place in conventional oven for 5 minutes on broil to brown and crisp the crust.

When warming any type of bread, place first on a paper towel or cloth napkin so moisture trapped between bread and oven floor will be absorbed. Remember bread will toughen if over-heated. One roll may be warmed in only 8-12 seconds.

Crusty Yeast Bread

To get a crusty bread, brush loaves with a mixture of 1 beaten egg and 1 tablespoon water after making bread out into loaves and before topping with sesame seeds. Also place a small container of hot water in a conventional oven before baking or browning.

Yield 4 loaves

3 packages of active dry yeast
2 cups warm water (110°F - 115°F.)
4 teaspoons salt
1 cup Miller's Bran (or unsifted, unprocessed whole wheat flour)
6-7 cups bread flour
1 recipe of Bread Starter

In larger mixer bowl, dissolve yeast in warm water and stir in salt. Add 2 cups flour to make a thin batter and beat on high speed for 3 minutes. Add Bread Starter and stir to blend. Stir in remaining flour making a stiff dough. Pour onto lightly floured surface and knead until smooth and elastic, about 20-25 minutes if doing by hand. If using a mixer with a dough hook, knead 8-10 minutes. If using a food processor divide dough into 4-5 batches, processing 30 seconds and checking. Process in 15-second bursts until the desired consistency is reached. Dough should bounce back when touched. Divide dough into 4 different batches.

After shaping place bread on sheet or dish that has been sprinkled with cornmeal. Brush bread with egg wash mixture (1 egg and 1 tablespoon water) and top with sesame seed. Cover with plastic wrap and let rise in warm place until double, 45-60 minutes. If cooking conventionally, bake in a 400°F oven for 20-25 minutes, rearranging midway through cooking time. If cooking all of bread in microwave, use 9 inch glass pie plates that are well greased. Place a glass in the center and dough around edges. Since this recipe makes a large batch of bread, it is nice to cook a loaf or two conventionally. If microwaving, cook each dish of bread for 5-7 minutes on 50% power; then freeze them to be browned and finished cooking later conventionally.

Bread Starter

Soured batter gives this bread a special flavor.

1 package active dry yeast
1 cup warm water (110°F - 115°F.)
2 cups all-purpose flour

Dissolve yeast in warm water and stir in flour until a thick batter is formed. Let stand at room temperature 24 hours or until batter has soured. (You may speed the souring process by microwaving for 5 minutes at 10% power several times during this period).

Onion Flat Bread
Savory accompaniment for soup, salad or cheese.
Tastes like potato cakes!

Serves 4-6

1/4 cup butter
2 cups diced yellow onion
1 3/4 cup flour (Half of this may be whole wheat if desired)
1 1/4 teaspoon salt
1/2 cup cold water
2 slices of bacon and drippings

Sauté butter and onion for 3-4 minutes on HIGH. Cook bacon slices 2-3 minutes until crisp. (Drain, crumble and set aside.) Mix flour, salt and water with onion and butter mixture. Add bacon drippings and crumbled up bacon. Drop by spoonfulls onto a browning tray that has been preheated 6-7 minutes. Cook for 1 minute on HIGH and turn with spatula. Cook an additional 1 minute and serve warm.

English Muffin Loaf
Cooks in 6 1/2 minutes with all the
nooks and crannies as traditional!

5 cups unsifted flour
1 cup Miller's Bran
2 packages active dry yeast
1 tablespoon sugar
2 teaspoons salt
1/2 teaspoon baking soda
2 cups milk
3 tablespoons cornmeal

Place in large mixing bowl, 3 cups flour, Miller's Bran, undissolved yeast, sugar, salt and baking soda. Heat milk in microwave for 1 1/2 - 2 minutes on HIGH until very warm (120°F - 130°F). Add to dry ingredients and beat well. Stir in remaining flour to make a stiff batter. Prepare two standard loaf glass dishes by lightly greasing and sprinkling with cornmeal. Spoon bread dough into loaf dishes. Sprinkle tops with meal if desired. Cover tightly with plastic wrap that has first been oiled to prevent bread from sticking to wrap. Let rise 45 minutes in a warm place, free from draft. If speed rising is desired, place both loaves in microwave for 12 minutes on 10% power and let stand until double in bulk.

Remove plastic and microwave each loaf for 6 1/2 minutes on 50% power. Allow to stand 5 minutes before removing from dish. Cool. Slice and toast if desired, but it's yummy as is with butter!!

👹 For a different taste delight, try adding 2 tablespoons grated orange rind.

Simply Scrumptious
Cakes

Cakes
Scratch Cakes

"Cake Mix" Cakes

Fillings - Frostings - Icings

General Guidelines

Microwave baked cakes are lighter, moister and more tender than conventional cakes. They microwave in one-sixth to one-third the time needed conventionally.

Dish Preparation. No preparation is needed if the cake is to be served from the dish. If the cake is to be removed from the dish, line the bottom of dish with 2 layers of waxed paper or brown paper for easy removal. When baking a bundt cake, plain or fluted, grease the dish well with oil, butter, shortening or spray coating and coat with granulated sugar or cracker crumbs (graham, vanilla wafers or dry toasted bread crumbs). Never use flour for coating; it will become sticky and lumpy during cooking.

Baking Dish. Always think "round" for more even cooking results. Round dishes allow more even cooking than square ones. When square dishes are required, as when baking brownies or other cake squares, place a triangle of aluminum foil over each corner to "shield" it from overcooking. Rectangular dishes are not recommended for most even cooking results. Bundt and ring dishes give good results. If you do not have a glass or plastic tube cake dish, you can create one by inverting a 2 or 3-inch diameter glass or jar in a 3 or 4-quart round casserole or heat tempered glass bowl.

Baking. Fill the dish no more than 1/2 full. Use excess batter for cupcakes. Because of the short baking time, microwaved cakes will not brown. By using frostings, glazes, sauces and toppings, cakes may look appealing and quite often no different than conventionally baked. Bake cake layers separately, one at a time. Cakes are often microwaved at a reduced power level: 50%-70% to rise, and finished on HIGH to set the batter.

Testing for Doneness. As in conventional baking, cakes are done when a toothpick inserted near the center comes out clean, or when the top springs back when lightly pressed with a finger. The cake will usually start coming away from the edge of the dish. Unlike conventional cakes, the microwave cake should always appear slightly moist on top after baking. There should be a damp spot in the center. This moisture will disappear when the cake stands 2 or 3 minutes. If it does not, touch the damp spot with your finger. Sometimes the dampness you see is only moisture on the surface that has not evaporated. If so, it will usually stick to your finger and you can see the "done" cake beneath. If you continue cooking until the damp spot disappears, the cake will be overcooked and tough.

Standing time. Consider standing time part of the cooking process. After taking the cake from the oven, let it stand directly on the countertop 5-10 minutes. This helps the cake complete baking on the bottom. Never use a cooling rack. If you are uncertain about doneness when you test the cake, take it out of the oven and test again after standing time. The cake may be put back in the oven and baked more after standing time, if needed. Cover the cake with waxed paper or plastic wrap during standing time and after the cake is inverted, until it cools, to retain moisture in the cake. (You may want to leave the cake dish inverted on top of the cake while it is cooling.)

Converting Conventional Recipes to Microwaving. Yellow, chocolate or spice cakes convert well. Add an extra egg to a 1 or 2-egg cake. Reduce the liquid in a 3-egg cake by about 1/3. White cakes toughen when microwaved. When converting a white cake recipe, substitute 1 whole egg for 2 egg whites. Angel and sponge cakes cannot be microwave baked successfully because they require dry heat. They will rise, but will not develop the crust needed to hold their shape when removed from the oven.

Mary's Sour Cream Pound Cake

2 sticks butter
3 cups sugar
3 cups flour
1/4 teaspoon soda
1/2 teaspoon baking powder
1 cup sour cream
6 eggs
2 teaspoons flavoring (vanilla, lemon, almond, your preference)

Cream butter and sugar. Add eggs and beat until light and fluffy. Sift dry ingredients together and add to sugar mixture alternately with sour cream. Add flavoring. Pour into prepared 12-cup bundt dish (greased generously and coated with graham cracker crumbs). Microwave on 70% power for 15-18 minutes or until done. Cover with waxed paper and let stand 10-15 minutes on countertop. Invert.

Variations: Sour Cream Pound Cake is a good basic recipe. Delicious variations of pound cake may be made by following this basic recipe and making the following additions and substitutions.

Coconut Pound Cake: Fold in 2 cups grated fresh coconut and flavor the cake with 1 teaspoon coconut extract and 1 teaspoon almond extract.

Betty's Chocolate Pound Cake: Add 1/3 cup cocoa to dry ingredients.

Peanut Butter Pound Cake: Substitute 1/2 cup peanut butter for sour cream. Use 1 cup light brown sugar, firmly packed, and 2 cups granulated sugar instead of 3 cups granulated.

Brown Sugar Pound Cake: Instead of 3 cups sugar use 1 pound light brown sugar and 1 cup white sugar. Also add 1 cup finely chopped walnuts. After baked and inverted from dish, top with Walnut Glaze. To make glaze, cream 1 cup sifted powdered sugar and 2 tablespoons butter, Add 6 tablespoons cream, 1/2 teaspoon vanilla and 1/2 cup chopped walnuts. Blend well. After baking cake, invert from dish and top with Walnut Glaze.

Strawberry Pound Cake: Substitute 1 cup puréed fresh strawberries for sour cream. If using frozen, sweetened strawberries, reduce sugar to 2 3/4 cups.

Chocolate Sheet Cake

Makes a 9-inch square

1 cup flour
1 cup sugar
1/4 teaspoon salt
1/4 cup oil
1/2 stick butter
1/2 cup cocoa
1/3 cup water
1/4 cup buttermilk
1/2 teaspoon each baking soda and vanilla
1 egg

Combine flour, sugar and salt. Combine water, oil, butter and cocoa and microwave on HIGH 3 to 4 minutes to boiling. Pour over dry ingredients and mix. Add remaining ingredients, beating well. Pour into 9-inch square dish. Shield corners with foil. Microwave on 50% power 6 minutes and HIGH 2-6 minutes till done. Let stand directly on countertop 5-10 minutes. While cake is standing prepare frosting and frost cake while hot.

Frosting:

1/2 stick butter
2 tablespoons cocoa
3 tablespoons milk
1/2 pound powdered sugar
1/2 cup chopped nuts

Combine butter, cocoa, milk and vanilla and microwave on HIGH 2-3 minutes until it boils. Add powdered sugar and beat. Add nuts and spread on hot cake.

Date Nut Party Cake

Makes 1 (8-inch) layer

1/2 cup dates
1/2 cup boiling water
1/2 teaspoon soda
1/2 cup mayonnaise
1/2 cup sugar
1 egg
1 cup flour
1/4 teaspoon cinnamon
1/2 cup walnuts, finely chopped
1 tablespoon cocoa

Combine dates, water and soda and set aside. Beat mayonnaise and sugar. Add all remaining ingredients including date mixture. Beat 2 minutes. Spread in an 8-inch baking dish. Microwave on 50% power for 6 minutes and HIGH 2-5 minutes. Cover with wax paper. Let stand directly on countertop 10 minutes. Frost with Orange Fluff Frosting or serve with whipped cream.

Fruit cakes will require longer baking time than other cakes since the batter is dense.

Graham Cracker Cake

Makes one 9-inch square

1/2 cup sugar
1/4 cup butter
2 eggs
1 teaspoon baking powder
20 graham crackers, crushed
1/4 cup flour
1/2 cup milk
1/2 cup chopped nuts
1/2 teaspoon vanilla

Mix together baking powder and crumbs. Cream butter and sugar. Add eggs and vanilla. Add dry ingredients alternately with milk. Stir in nuts. Pour into greased 8-inch square dish. Shield corners with foil. Microwave on HIGH 5-6 minutes. Cover with plastic wrap and let stand 10 minutes on countertop. Spread topping on while cake is hot.

Topping: Combine 1/2 cup crushed pineapple, drained and 1/2 cup sugar. Microwave on HIGH until clear.

Winky's Pineapple Sheet Cake

Makes two 8-inch sheets

1/2 cup shortening
1 cup sugar
2 eggs
1 teaspoon vanilla
1 (20-ounce) can crushed pineapple, in heavy syrup, undrained
2 cups flour
1 teaspoon baking soda
1/2 teaspon salt
1 1/2 teaspoon baking powder

Cream shortening and sugar. Add eggs, vanilla and pineapple. Sift dry ingredients together and stir into the sugar mixture. Spread in two 8-inch square dishes. Shield corners. Microwave one at a time on 50% power for 6 minutes and HIGH 2-6 minutes until done. Let stand directly on countertop 5-10 minutes. While cake is standing prepare frosting and frost cake while hot.

Frosting: Cream 1 pound sifted confectioners sugar and 8 ounces of cream cheese. (The cheese may be microwaved on HIGH about 45 seconds to soften.) Add 1/2 to 1 cup chopped nuts. Spread on cake.

Toasted coconut. Spread 1 cup grated coconut on a pie plate and microwave uncovered on HIGH for about 1 minute. Stir and cook 1 minute longer.

The cake top can be soft and sticky. To dry the surface and help the frosting stick to the cake, sprinkle about 1 tablespoon cracker crumbs or granulated sugar on each layer after baking and before frosting.

Hummingbird Cake
A yummy cake!

Makes one 9-inch layer

3/4 cup flour
3/4 cup sugar
1 teaspoon each, baking powder, cinnamon and vanilla
1/2 teaspoon soda
2 eggs
1/2 cup cooking oil
1 banana, chopped
1/2 cup pecans, chopped
1/2 cup crushed canned pineapple with juice

Place all ingredients in mixing bowl. Blend at low speed, then at medium speed 2 minutes. Spread batter in a 9-inch round dish. Microwave on 50% power for 6 minutes and HIGH 2-6 minutes until done. Cover with wax paper and let stand directly on countertop 5-10 minutes. Cool and frost with Cream Cheese Frosting. See page 151.

 To make a torte, freeze the cake, split each layer horizontally and frost.

 Hummingbird Bundt Cake. Double recipe and bake in a prepared 12-cup ring cake dish (greased and dusted with graham cracker crumbs) 12 minutes on 50% power and 1-8 minutes on HIGH. Frost with Cream Cheese Frosting.

Italian Cream Cake

Makes one 9-inch layer

1 stick butter
3/4 cup sugar
3/4 cup flour
1/2 teaspoon soda
2 eggs
1 teaspoon each, vanilla and baking powder
1/2 cup coconut
1/2 cup chopped nuts
1/2 cup buttermilk

Cream butter and sugar. Add eggs. Combine dry ingredients and add to butter mixture alternately with buttermilk. Fold in coconut and nuts. Add vanilla. Spread in a 9-inch square dish and microwave on 50% power for 6 minutes and HIGH 2-6 minutes, or until done. Frost with Cream Cheese Nut Frosting. See page 151.

 To reheat individual portions of frosted or unfrosted cake, place each piece on a plate. Cover with waxed paper. Microwave on HIGH 10-15 seconds or until heated.

 Clear glass baking dishes enable you to check the bottom for uncooked batter.

Quick Coffee Cake

Yield: 8-inch cake

1/4 cup butter
1/2 cup sugar
1 egg
1/2 teaspoon vanilla extract
1/2 cup sour cream
1 cup flour
1/2 teaspoon baking powder
1/2 teaspoon baking soda

Topping:

1/3 cup brown sugar	dash of salt
3 tablespoons butter	1/4 teaspoon ground cinnamon
2 tablespoons flour	1/4 cup chopped nuts

Cream butter and sugar. Add egg and vanilla, beating well. Blend in remaining ingredients. Pour into baking dish.

Mix all of topping ingredients together blending with a pastry blender or 2 knives. Sprinkle mixture over top of coffee cake. Microwave on 50% power for 8 minutes and on HIGH 1-3 minutes.

Let stand in dish 3-5 minutes. Invert on platter so strudel topping will be visible.

Fresh Apple Pound Cake

1 1/4 cups cooking oil
2 cups sugar
3 eggs
3 cups flour
1 teaspoon each salt and baking soda
2 teaspoons vanilla extract
3 large apples, grated
1 cup finely chopped pecans

Combine oil, sugar, and eggs; beat at medium speed for 3 minutes. Add combined flour, salt, soda and vanilla. Fold in apples and pecans. Bake in prepared 12-cup ring cake dish. Microwave on 50% power 12 minutes and HIGH 1-8 minutes. Let stand, covered with waxed paper, on countertop 10 minutes. Invert and glaze.

Glaze: Combine 3/4 cup butter and 1 1/2 cups light brown sugar in a deep bowl. Microwave on 70% power until mixture begins to boil. Add 1/3 cup evaporated milk and continue to microwave on 70% power until mixture boils again. Cook until thickened. Add 2 teaspoons vanilla. Cool and spread on cake. (This cooks quickly.)

Leftover toppings and icings may be refrigerated. Make them "spreadable" by microwaving a few seconds.

Opening the oven door will not cause the cake to "fall" as it sometimes does conventionally since there is no heat in the microwave oven.

Wanda's Vanilla Wafer Cake

2 sticks butter
2 cups sugar
6 eggs
1 (7-ounce) package coconut
1 (12-ounce) box vanilla wafers, crushed
1/3 cup milk
1 cup pecans, chopped

Cream butter and sugar, add eggs. Add remaining ingredients. Pour into prepared 12-cup tube dish (greased and sprinkled with cracker crumbs). Microwave on 50% power for 9 minutes then on HIGH 3-6 minutes or until done.

Quick Cake
As quick as a mix!

Makes one 8-inch layer

6 tablespoons butter
1 cup sugar
1 1/2 cups flour
2 teaspoons baking powder
1/4 teaspoon salt
2 eggs
1 cup milk
1 teaspoon vanilla

Beat all ingredients together and pour into an 8-inch dish. Microwave on 50% power for 6 minutes and HIGH 2-5 minutes. Let stand directly on countertop to cool.

CUPCAKES: Cupcakes are especially easy and quick to microwave and fun for "very young cooks." For best results always use 2 paper liners in each cup to absorb excess moisture. The cupcakes cook so fast that moisture pulled out of the batter does not have time to evaporate. The two layers of paper absorb some of the moisture so that the cupcakes are not soggy. Fill 1/3 to 1/2 full with batter. If using custard cups, arrange them in a circular pattern in the oven. After cooking, remove the cupcakes from custard cups or baking dish as soon as they are done. Let cool on a rack 2-3 minutes. Since cake doesn't brown, use frosting, crumb, nut or spice toppings for eye appeal. Use these cooking times as a guide.

Quantity	HIGH POWER
1	25-30 seconds
2	3/4 - 1 1/4 minutes
3	1 - 1 1/2 minutes
4	1 1/2 - 2 minutes
5	2 - 2 1/2 minutes
6	2 - 3 minutes

🐢 If your oven requires rotating food for even cooking, simplify turning cupcakes by placing them on a microwave safe plate or tray. The plate can be rotated instead of having to reposition each cupcake.

Delicious Cake Mix Cakes

Following are several recipes using mixes. Prepare these cakes by following these directions for mixing and baking: Combine all ingredients (unless otherwise directed) and mix 1-2 minutes. Spread batter in a prepared 12-cup bundt dish and microwave for 12 minutes on 50% power and on HIGH 1-8 minutes until done. Let stand 10 minutes directly on countertop covered with waxed paper or plastic wrap. Invert and cool, covered with waxed paper or leave the baking dish inverted over the cake to prevent excessive evaporation of moisture. Frost or glaze as recipe instructs. (If the cake is to be sliced into layers for frosting, you may want to freeze the cake first so that it can be more easily sliced.)

Strawberry Cake: 1 (18 1/2-ounce) package yellow cake mix, 4 eggs, 1/2 cup oil, 1 (10-ounce) carton frozen strawberries. Bake, cool, and slice into 3 layers.

>**Icing:** 1 (10-ounce) carton strawberries, 1 (3 3/4-ounce) package instant vanilla pudding, 1 (9-ounce) carton whipped topping. Combine and spread between layers.

Harvey Wallbanger Cake: 1 (18 1/2-ounce) package orange cake mix, 1 (3 3/4-ounce) package instant vanilla pudding, 3/4 cup orange juice, 1/2 cup oil, 4 eggs, 1/4 cup water, 1/4 cup Galliano.

>**Glaze:** 1 cup powdered sugar, 1 tablespoon orange juice, 1 tablespoon vodka, 1 tablespoon Galliano, 1 tablespoon white corn syrup. Combine ingredients and drizzle over cake.

Orange Torte Cake: 1 (18 1/2-ounce) yellow cake mix, 4 eggs, 1/2 cup oil, 1 (11-ounce) can mandarin oranges. Bake, cool, slice into 3 layers.

>**Icing:** 1 (9-ounce) carton whipped topping, 1 (3 3/4-ounce) package instant vanilla pudding, 1 (8 1/2-ounce) can crushed pineapple and 1/2 cup chopped pecans or 1/2 cup coconut. Combine ingredients and spread between layers.

Prune Spice Cake: 1 (18 1/2-ounce) package deluxe spice cake mix, 1 (3 3/4-ounce) package vanilla instant pudding mix, 1 (7 3/4-ounce) jar junior prunes with tapioca, 3/4 cup water, 1/2 cup oil, 4 eggs, 1 teaspoon lemon extract.

>**Glaze:** 1/2 medium banana, 1 tablespoon lemon juice, 2 cups powdered sugar. Mash banana and add lemon juice. Gradually add powdered sugar, beating until smooth. Microwave on HIGH 1-2 minutes and drizzle on cake.

Double Chocolate Chip Cake: 1 (18 1/2-ounce) Super Moist Chocolate cake mix, 1 cup sour cream, 3 eggs, 2/3 cup water, 6 ounces chocolate chips, and 1/2 cup chopped nuts. Combine mix, sour cream, eggs, and water as directed above and fold in chips and nuts.

Rum Cake: 1 (18 1/2-ounce) package yellow cake mix, 1 (3 3/4-ounce) package vanilla instant pudding, 1/2 cup Meyer's dark rum, 1/2 cup water, 1/2 cup oil, 4 eggs, 1/2 cup pecans.

> **Glaze:** 1/4 cup rum, 1/4 cup water, 1/2 cup butter, 1 cup sugar. Combine water, butter and sugar and microwave on HIGH until it boils and sugar is dissolved. Add rum. Cool until it begins to thicken and pour over cake.

Black Russian Cake: 1 (18 1/2-ounce) package chocolate cake mix, 1/2 cup oil, 1 (3 3/4-ounce) package instant chocolate pudding, 4 eggs, 3/4 cup strong coffee, 3/4 cup combined Kahlua and crème de cocoa.

> **Glaze:** 1 cup powdered sugar, 1 tablespoon strong coffee, 1 tablespoon Kahlua, 1 tablespoon crème de cocoa. Combine ingredients and drizzle over cake.

Carrot Cake: 1 (18 1/2-ounce) package yellow cake mix, 1 (3-ounce) package vanilla instant pudding, 4 eggs, 1/3 cup oil, 3 cups grated carrots, 1/2 cup raisins, 1/2 cup chopped walnuts, 2 teaspoons cinnamon, pinch salt. Ice with Cream Cheese Nut icing. See page 151.

Very Berry Cake: 1 (18 1/2-ounce) package yellow cake mix, 1 (15-ounce) can blueberries in heavy syrup, drained and liquid reserved, 8 ounces plain yogurt or sour cream, 4 eggs. Combine mix, yogurt and eggs. Carefully fold in blueberries.

> **Sauce:** 1 cup reserved blueberry syrup, 1 tablespoon cornstarch, 1/4 cup sugar. Combine sugar and cornstarch. Add syrup and microwave on HIGH 3-5 minutes until thickened.

Cherry Chocolate Cake: 1 (18 1/2-ounce) package devil's food cake mix, 1 (21-ounce) can cherry pie filling, divided in half, 1 teaspoon ground cinnamon, 3 eggs, 1/2 cup water, 1/3 cup vegetable oil. Pour half the pie filling in the bottom of bundt dish. Add the other half with the other ingredients. Serve whipped cream with this cake.

Pumpkin Cake: 1 (18 1/2-ounce) package yellow cake mix, 2 teaspoons pumpkin pie spice, 1 can canned pumpkin, 1/2 cup water, 3 eggs.

> **Glaze:** 1 cup powdered sugar, 1 1/2 ounces cream cheese, 1 tablespoon milk, 1 teaspoon vanilla. Blend ingredients and spoon over cooled cake.

Pistachio Cake: 1 (18 1/2-ounce) package white cake mix, 1 (3 3/4-ounce) package instant pistachio pudding, 3 eggs, 1 cup cooking oil, 1 cup sour cream, 1/2 cup chopped nuts. Cook, cook and slice into 3 layers.

> **Icing:** 1 (3 3/4-ounce) package pistachio pudding, 1 (13-ounce) carton whipped topping, adding milk to thin to spreading consistency.

Cake Mixes

Because commercial cake mixes have a stabilizer added, cake mix batter may be stored covered in the refrigerator several weeks or frozen several months. To defrost batter, microwave covered with plastic wrap 5 minutes on 30%-40% power. Remove plastic wrap and bake. A 1-layer batter may be cooked in a 6-cup ring dish. A 2-layer batter may be cooked in a 12-cup ring dish on 50% power for 12 minutes and HIGH 1-8 minutes or until done. When baking a 2-layer cake from a mix, fill 2 dishes 1/2 full and make about 1/2 dozen cupcakes. Microwave layers separately on 50% power for 6 minutes and HIGH 2-6 minutes or until done. Square dishes hold more batter than round ones and require a minute or two longer cooking.

Coconut Sheet Cake

Makes two 8-inch squares

1 (18 1/2-ounce) yellow cake mix
1 (13-ounce) carton whipped topping
Syrup:
14-ounce package coconut
1 cup sugar
2 cups milk

Prepare cake according to package directions. Pour into two 8-inch square dishes, shield corners, and microwave one at a time on 50% power 6 minutes, then HIGH 2-6 minutes until done. Let stand 10 minutes on countertop. Meanwhile prepare the syrup. Combine syrup ingredients and microwave on HIGH 5-6 minutes or to boiling. Stir to dissolve sugar. Punch holes in cake with a fork and pour syrup over. Cool 30 minutes. Then spread whipped topping over cake and refrigerate overnight or longer before serving.

Quick Any-Flavor Cake

Makes 2 layers or a bundt cake

1 (18 1/2-ounce) package cake mix
1 (21-ounce) can pie filling, or
   1 (10-ounce) package frozen fruit, or
   1 1/2 cups fresh or frozen fruit, mashed
4 eggs
1/2 cup sour cream or 1/2 cup oil

Mix all ingredients and spread in a prepared 12-cup bundt dish. Microwave on 50% power for 12 minutes and HIGH 1-8 minutes or until done. Let stand 10 minutes, invert and frost when cool. (Or spread batter in two 9-inch round dishes and microwave each layer separately on 50% power for 6 minutes and on HIGH 2-6 minutes or until done.)

Try these flavor combinations: chocolate cake/cherry pie filling; yellow cake/pumpkin or any fruit pie filling; lemon or orange cake mix/1-pound can whole cranberry sauce; gingerbread/brandied mincemeat; yellow cake/fresh or frozen peaches.

Shortcake

Simply Scrumptious when served with fresh fruits
and whipped cream!

1 1/2 cups flour
1 teaspoon baking powder
Dash salt
6 tablespoons sugar
1/4 cup butter
1 egg
1 1/2 tablespoons cognac
1 tablespoon grated lemon or orange peel

Sift flour, baking powder and salt together. Add sugar and butter, and work
with fingers till smooth. Add egg and cognac and work into mixture. Add
citrus rind. Shape dough into a ball. Flatten to about an 8-inch circle. Brush
with egg wash and score with fork. Microwave on 50% power for 5 minutes
and HIGH 3-4 minutes. If possible, let mellow at room temperature overnight. (To make egg wash, combine 1 egg and 2 tablespoons water.)

For a browned shortcake, put under the conventional broiler a few
minutes.

Quick Coconut Cake

Makes a tall layer cake

1 (18 1/2-ounce) box Duncan Hines Golden Butter cake mix
2 cups sugar
2 cups sour cream
2 (9-ounce) packages frozen coconut, thawed
1 1/2 cups whipped topping

Mix cake according to package directions, using two 8 or 9-inch layer
dishes. Microwave layers separately, cooking each on 50% power for 6
minutes then HIGH 2-6 minutes. Let cool on countertop 10 minutes.

Split each layer in half horizontally. Combine sour cream, sugar and
coconut. Chill. Reserve 1 cup sour cream mixture for frosting. Spread remainder between layers of cake. Combine reserved sour cream mixture with
whipped topping. Blend until smooth. Spread on top and sides of cake.
Store in air-tight container in refrigerator 3 days before serving.

Lemon cake mix is also very good in this recipe.

Cake Fillings

*Cake fillings are basically thick sweet sauces. See "sauces" in the
Desserts chapter of Simply Scrumptious for additional filling ideas. To use
a sauce recipe as a cake filling, add a little more thickening or cook to a
thicker consistency. Cool before spreading on cake. Also see "puddings".*

Coconut Filling

1 (13-ounce) can evaporated milk
1 cup sugar
1/2 cup butter
3 tablespoons flour
1 teaspoon vanilla
1 (3 1/2-ounce) can or 1 1/2 cups flaked coconut
1/2 cup chopped pecans (optional)

Combine milk, sugar, butter, flour and vanilla together in a deep bowl. Microwave on 50%-70% power until thickened, about 5-10 minutes. Stir several times during cooking. Stir in coconut and nuts. Cool completely before using.

Chocolate Filling

1 1/3 cups sugar
1/4 teaspoon cream of tartar
2/3 cup water
8 egg yolks
1/2 cup dark cocoa
2 teaspoons vanilla
1 pound butter

Combine sugar, cream of tartar and water and microwave on HIGH to soft-boil stage (240°F). Meanwhile, beat egg yolks 3-4 minutes. Pour hot syrup into eggs in a slow steady stream while continuing to beat. Continue beating 10-15 minutes until smooth thick cream. Beat in cocoa and vanilla. Then beat in butter a tablespoon at a time. Refrigerate till ready to use.

Shirley's Caramel Icing

3 cups sugar
3/4 cup half-and-half or evaporated milk
1 cup butter

Combine 2 cups sugar, half-and-half, and butter in a deep bowl and microwave at 70% power about 5-6 minutes to dissolve sugar and melt butter. In a separate dish, combine remaining cup of sugar and 1 tablespoon water. Microwave on HIGH 3-6 minutes or until sugar caramalizes (becomes brown and liquid). Watch carefully after first 2 minutes of cooking. Add caramalized sugar to the first mixture and microwave on 70% power for 15-20 minutes or until mixture reaches about 225°F, very soft ball stage. Cool a few minutes and beat with electric mixer until thickened and smooth. Add chopped nuts if desired.

Microwaved cakes are very tender. You may prefer to slightly freeze the cake layers before you split them.

Cream Cheese Frosting

Yields icing for 1 layer (1 1/2 cups)

4 ounces softened cream cheese
3 tablespoons softened butter
1/2 pound powdered sugar
1 teaspoon vanilla

Blend ingredients and beat until light and fluffy. Thin with a little milk or cream, if desired.

Cream Cheese Nut Frosting. Add 1/2 cup chopped nuts to Cream Cheese Frosting.

To use as a glaze on bundt cakes or coffee cakes, microwave on HIGH about one minute. Then drizzle over cake.

ICING QUICKIE. Combine 1 (9-ounce) carton whipped topping, 1 (3-ounce) package instant pudding and 1 cup canned or frozen fruit with liquid.

Five-Minute Frosting

Frosts two 9-inch layers

1 cup sugar
1/2 cup water
1/4 teaspoon cream of tartar
Dash salt
2 egg whites
1 teaspoon vanilla

Combine sugar, water, cream of tartar and salt in deep bowl. Microwave on 70% power for 4-5 minutes or until mixture boils. Meanwhile, beat egg whites until soft peaks form. Gradually pour in hot syrup, beat about 5 minutes or until thick and fluffy. Blend in vanilla.

Variations:

Seafoam Frosting: Substitute light brown sugar for white. It's Simply Scrumptious on Date Nut Party Cake, spice or apple cake.

Pineapple: Substitute pineapple juice for water. Fold in 2 teaspoons grated lemon rind.

Pink Cloud: Fold in 1/4 cup well drained, finely chopped maraschino cherries.

Lemon: Decrease water 1 tablespoon and add 3 tablespoons lemon juice. After beating, fold in 1 teaspoon lemon rind and 1/2 teaspoon almond extract.

Chocolate: Fold in 1 square unsweetened chocolate melted. (Microwave at 70% power 2-3 minutes).

Marshmallow: Fold in 6-8 marshmallows, quartered.

Peppermint: Fold in 1/2 cup crushed peppermint candy.

Orange Fluff: Substitute orange juice for water. Fold in 2 teaspoons grated orange rind (optional).

Crème Au Beurre
A Rich, Delicious Buttercream Filling!

1 cup sugar
1/3 cup hot water
1/4 teaspoon cream of tartar
8 egg yolks
1 cup butter

Microwave sugar, water and cream of tarter on HIGH to soft-ball stage (240ºF) about 5-10 minutes. Meanwhile, beat egg yolks until light and fluffy. Pour syrup very gradually into the egg yolks, beating constantly. Continue beating until the mixture is cool and very thick and fluffy. Add softened butter, a tablespoon at a time, continuing to beat.

To vary the flavor of Crème Au Beurre, beat in 3 tablespoons cognac, rum, liqueur or fruit purée after butter has been added.

Lemon Cheese Filling

6 egg yolks
1 1/2 cups sugar
1 stick butter
4 lemons, juice and grated rind

Combine ingredients and microwave on HIGH 5-8 minutes or until thickened, stirring several times.

Instant Chocolate Frosting

Makes 1 1/2 cups

1 (14-ounce) can sweetened condensed milk
1 (6-ounce) package chocolate chips

Microwave on 70% power 2-3 minutes. Stir until chips melt. Heat a few more seconds if needed to make a smooth mixture. Good especially on chocolate cake.

Best Ever Chocolate Icing

3 cups sugar
3/4 cup cocoa
3/4 cup evaporated milk
3/4 cup butter

Combine ingredients in a deep bowl and microwave on 70% power about 5-10 minutes or until mixture starts to thicken. Let cool at room temperature until lukewarm. Beat to spreading consistency.

Buttercream Frosting

Yields icing for two 8-inch layers

2 cups powdered sugar
1/2 teaspoon vanilla
3 tablespoons butter
1-2 tablespoons cream

Microwave butter and cream on 50% power for 1-2 minutes or until bubbling. Add sugar and vanilla and beat until smooth. Add a few drops cream if needed to achieve spreading consistency.

Variations:

Fudge: Add 2 ounces unsweetened chocolate to butter and cream. Microwave on 50% power 3-4 minutes to melt chocolate.

Coffee: Add 1/2 teaspoon instant coffee to butter before microwaving.

Maple: Substitute maple flavoring for vanilla.

Lemon: Substitute 1 tablespoon lemon juice and 1 tablespoon cream for cream. Add 1 teaspoon grated lemon peel and 2-3 drops yellow food coloring.

Orange: Substitute orange juice for cream and add 1 teaspoon grated orange rind.

Peanut Butter Frosting: Add 2 teaspoons peanut butter to butter before microwaving.

Butterscotch: Add 1/3 cup brown sugar to butter before microwaving and cook an additional minute or two to dissolve sugar.

Japanese Fruit Cake Filling

3 cups sugar
1 1/2 cups coconut milk or water
6 tablespoons cornstarch
Juice of 2 lemons
4-5 cups fresh grated coconut
Rind of 1 lemon

Combine sugar, coconut milk or water and juice with cornstarch; microwave for 4-6 minutes until thickened. Cool and add coconut and rind.

Pineapple Cake Filling

Yield

1 cup crushed pineapple
3/4 cup sugar
3 tablespoons flour
2 tablespoons butter

Melt butter for 30 seconds on HIGH. Add flour and stir to blend. Add crushed pineapple and sugar and microwave for 3-4 minutes, until thick stirring midway during cooking time. Very tasty over a layer cake.

Apricot-Pineapple Filling

1 cup crushed pineapple
1 cup minced dried apricots
1/2 cup sugar
3 tablespoons orange juice
1 cup flaked coconut

Combine pineapple, apricots, sugar and orange juice in a 1-quart measuring cup. Cook for 4-5 minutes on HIGH, stirring several times. Remove from oven and cover with plastic wrap. Allow to stand 5 minutes. Add coconut and spread over an 8-inch cake while still warm. Garnish with whipped cream.

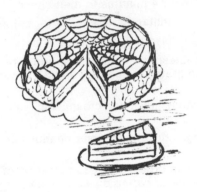

Sprinkle flavored gelatin over warm cake to form a colored glaze.

Make pastry cut-outs for garnishing pies. Roll out left-over pastry dough to 1/8 inch thickness. Cut into desired shapes. Sprinkle with a mixture of 1 teaspoon sugar and 1/8 teaspoon cinnamon. Arrange in circular pattern on baking sheet or waxed paper. Microwave 2-4 minutes or until dry and puffy. Loosen from waxed paper while warm.

Shell pecans or walnuts easily and with less breakage. Microwave 2 cups of nuts and 1 cup tap water in covered dish on HIGH for 1 1/2-2 minutes.

Simply Scrumptious
Pies & Desserts

Pies & Desserts

General Guidelines

Fruit pie fillings have a Simply Scrumptious fresh flavor and texture because of their short cooking time. Cream fillings are simple to prepare since they do not have to be constantly stirred to prevent scorching as in conventional cooking. Conventional recipes usually need no ingredient changes for microwave use.

Pastry crusts. Always prebake the pie shell. To minimize pie crust shrinkage during microwaving, allow dough to rest 3-5 minutes before final shaping and do not stretch dough while putting into pie plate.

Allow crust to cool before adding fillings. Crusts become crisper during cooling. Check for doneness a minute before minimum suggested cooking time since crusts differ in thickness and moisture content. Pastry should be dry and opaque when done.

Double crust pies cannot be microwaved because the crust won't cook properly. There is too much steam and moisture from the filling for the upper crust to be dry and crisp. To give fruit pies the appearance of a top crust, use lattice or pastry cut-outs that have been microwaved separately. Crumb crusts adapt to microwaving without change in ingredients. Use less filling since it bubbles hard. A high fluted pastry edge helps contain the bubbling filling. Use a reduced power setting, 50% or 70% to reduce boil overs.

Whole Wheat Pastry

1/3 cup shortening
2 tablespoons butter
1 cup whole wheat flour
1/2 teaspoon salt
3 tablespoons cold water
1 tablespoon brown sugar (optional)

Cut shortening and butter into flour and salt with pastry blender until mixture forms coarse crumbs. Sprinkle water over mixture while stirring with a fork until mixture is moist enough to cling together. You may not need all the water. Place in a 9-inch pie plate and let rest 10 minutes to reduce shrinkage. Trim and crimp edges. Prick crust with fork. Microwave on HIGH 5-7 minutes. When done, crust will appear dry and opaque.

🍓 Use whole wheat pastry for cream, chiffon, mincemeat, apple, peach and other fruit pies.

Graham Cracker Crust

Makes 9-inch pie shell

1/4 cup butter
1 1/3 cups graham cracker crumbs
2 tablespons brown sugar (optional)

Microwave butter in pie plate on HIGH 45-60 seconds. Stir in crumbs and sugar. Press mixture against bottom and side of plate. Microwave on HIGH 1 1/2 minutes. Cool. (For a peanut graham crust, add 1/4 cup peanut butter. Fill with banana cream filling.)

Substitute crushed vanilla wafers, cereal crumbs, gingersnaps or chocolate wafers for graham cracker crumbs.

A Simply Scrumptious quick crust may be made by substituting short-bread cookie crumbs for graham cracker crumbs to make a crust for fruit filling or other filling you would ordinarily put in a pastry.

Oatmeal Crust

2 cups quick-cooking oats
1/3 cup packed brown sugar
1/2 cup butter
1/4 cup flour

Combine oats, butter, sugar, and flour and press firmly against bottom and sides of 9-inch pie plate. If possible, place an 8-inch pie plate on top of crumb mixture and press down. Microwave on HIGH 2-3 minutes. Again press crust against pie plate to re-shape. Allow to stand 5-10 minutes. Very good with chocolate cream pie filling.

Other Simply Scrumptious Crusts

PECAN CRUST: 1 cup flour, 2 tablespoons brown sugar, 1/2 cup butter, 3/4 cup chopped pecans. Mix with pastry blender until particles resemble coarse crumbs. Press on bottom and sides of a 9-inch pie plate. Microwave on HIGH 3-5 minutes.

CHOCOLATE COCONUT CRUST: 2 ounces unsweetened chocolate, 2 tablespoons butter, 2 tablespoons hot milk, 2/3 cup sifted confectioners sugar, 1 1/2 cups thin-flaked coconut, toasted or untoasted. Melt chocolate and butter by microwaving on 70% power 3-4 minutes. Add milk and sugar, stirring well. Add coconut. Spread in bottom and sides of buttered 9-inch pie plate. Chill until firm. (Do not freeze.) Fill with chiffon, cream pie filling or softened ice cream.

COCONUT CRUST: 1/2 cup melted butter, 1 (7-ounce) can coconut, 2 table-spoons flour, 1/2 cup chopped pecans. Microwave butter in 9-inch pie plate on HIGH 1/2 - 1 1/2 minutes. Mix in other ingredients. Press against bottom and sides of plate. Microwave on HIGH 2-3 minutes. Cool. Fill with cream filling or ice cream.

To crisp and renew the fresh flavor of day old cookies, crackers or chips, microwave uncovered on HIGH 5-15 seconds.

Banana Split Dessert

Base:
1/2 pound graham cracker crumbs
1 stick butter

Filling:
2 eggs
1 pound powdered sugar
1 stick butter

Topping:
3 large bananas
20-ounce can crushed pineapple, drained
1/2 cup chopped nuts
1/2 cup cherries, diced
9-ounce container of whipped topping

Prepare base by melting butter on HIGH about 1 minute and stirring into cracker crumbs. Press mixture into a 10 x 14-inch dish.

Prepare filling: Beat eggs, add butter and sugar. Mix for several minutes or until smooth. Pour over crust.

Topping: Cover filling with sliced bananas, then spread on crushed pineapple, whipped topping, and sprinkle on nuts and cherries. Refrigerate.

Crème De Menthe Pie

Makes 9-inch pie

3 cups miniature marshmallows
1/2 cup milk
1/4 cup crème de menthe
2 cups heavy cream, whipped
24 cream filled chocolate cookies (Oreos)
1/4 cup melted butter
Several drops green food coloring, if desired

To make crust, crush cookies (including frosting) thoroughly. Combine crumbs and butter. Press into 9-inch pie plate. Reserve 1/2 cup mixture for topping. Combine marshmallows, food coloring and milk in deep bowl. Microwave on HIGH 2 - 2 1/2 minutes or until marshmallows begin to puff. Stir until smooth. Stir in crème de menthe and mix well. Refrigerate about 30 minutes. Fold in whipped cream and pour into crust. Refrigerate at least 4 hours. Garnish with reserved crumbs.

Whipped topping may be used instead of whipping cream, but yields an entirely different consistency — a soft creamy texture that does not hold its shape. It must be frozen.

BRANDY ALEXANDER PIE: Substitute 1/4 cup dark crème de cocoa and 2 tablespoons brandy for crème de menthe.

KAHLUA PIE: Substitute 1/2 cup Kahlua and 1 teaspoon instant coffee for crème de menthe.

Rock Eagle Butterscotch-Date Pie

Pie shell, pastry or graham cracker
2 cups evaporated milk or half-and-half
6 tablespoons butter
4 egg yolks
3/4 cup light brown sugar
3 tablespoons cornstarch
2 tablespoons flour
Dash salt
1/2 cup chopped dates
1 teaspoon vanilla
Whipped cream and nuts to garnish

Heat milk and butter on HIGH 5 minutes. Combine sugar, cornstarch, flour, and salt; beat in egg yolks; then add to heated milk. Cook until thick, about 4-6 minutes on HIGH. Stir in dates and vanilla. Chill and pour into pie shell. Just before serving, garnish with whipped cream and sprinkle nuts on top.

Chocolate Fondue

1 ounce semisweet chocolate (or unsweetened, if you prefer)
1/2 cup whipping cream
2 tablespoons dark rum

Cook on HIGH about 2 - 2 1/2 minutes until melted and very hot. Stir several times. Use fresh fruit: pineapple, apple, orange, papaya, strawberries, grapes, bananas, or angel food cake or doughnut pieces for dipping.

To reheat, microwave on 50% power 30-45 seconds.

Pecan Cream Cheese Pie

Crust:
1 1/2 cups graham cracker crumbs
1 stick butter
1/3 cup finely chopped pecans

Filling:
2 (8 ounce) packages cream cheese
1 cup brown sugar
3/4 cup chopped pecans

Topping:
1 cup sour cream
2 tablespoons brown sugar
2 teaspoons vanilla

Combine crust ingredients and press into a 9-inch pie plate. Cook on HIGH 1 1/2 minutes. Microwave cream cheese on HIGH about 45 seconds to soften; beat in 1 cup sugar until smooth and creamy. Add nuts and spoon into pie shell. Cook on 50% power about 5 minutes. Mix topping ingredients and spoon over pie. Microwave on 50% power for 3 minutes. Cool and garnish with chopped pecans or pecan halves. Chill.

Chocomint Dessert
A Good Dessert for a Crowd.

Serves 16

Crust:

2 cups finely crushed chocolate wafers
1/2 cup butter

Green filling:

1 (13-ounce) can evaporated milk
1 (3-ounce) package lime-flavored gelatin
1 (8-ounce) package cream cheese
1 cup sugar
Several drops green food coloring

Chocolate Pie Filling:
  Recipe on page 167
1/4 cup finely crushed, hard peppermint candies,
  or peppermint flavoring to taste.

Prepare crust by microwaving butter on HIGH about 45 seconds to melt. Combine with crumbs; reserve 1/3 cup for topping. Press remainder over bottom of 9 x 13-inch dish.

To prepare the green filling, freeze evaporated milk in freezer tray until crystals form around the edges. Meanwhile, microwave 1 cup water for 2 - 2 1/2 minutes to boiling. Dissolve gelatin in water and let stand 30 minutes. Beat together cream cheese and sugar; gradually beat in gelatin and food coloring. Whip evaporated milk to soft peaks; fold in cheese mixture. Spread half over crust; chill 1 hour. Keep remaining mixture at room temperature. Make chocolate pie filling and stir in candy or flavoring. Cool. Spoon over green layer. Top with remaining cheese mixture. Sprinkle with crumbs. Chill.

White Chocolate Mousse
Simply Scrumptious with Fresh Strawberries!

Serves 8-10

10 ounces white chocolate
1/2 cup sugar
1/4 cup water
4 egg whites
1 tablespoon vanilla
2 tablespoons Cointreau
1 cup heavy cream

Break chocolate into small pieces. Microwave at 70% for 2-3 minutes or until chocolate melts. Prepare syrup by microwaving the sugar and water until soft boil stage, 230° F, about 5-10 minutes at 70%. Meanwhile, beat egg whites until soft peaks form. Pour in syrup while beating and continue beating until mixture is room temperature (Italian meringue). Fold in chocolate, cointreau and vanilla. Whip cream and fold into chocolate mixture. Freeze. Serve garnished with chocolate curls or fresh fruit.

Ice Cream Bombes

A bombe is a combination of 2 or more flavors of ice cream or sherbert, usually formed in a round mold or bowl. Microwaving simplifies and hastens the preparation of a bombe since the ice cream can be softened to the proper consistency in seconds. They are "easy and elegant" and can be made days in advance.

To prepare the mold or bowl, oil lightly and line with plastic wrap, smoothing out all wrinkles. Chill thoroughly.

Each layer must be put into the mold when soft enough to be spread (but not too soft) then frozen hard before the next layer is added.

Hard ice cream may be softened at 40% power. Allow 15-30 seconds for one pint, 30-45 seconds for one quart, 45-60 seconds for one-half gallon.

Elegant Bombe

Serves 8-10

This is a favorite. It has four layers: pistachio, vanilla, raspberry and ganache cream (fudge).

First layer: 1 quart good quality vanilla ice cream, 1/2 of a 3-ounce package pistachio pudding mix, 2/3 cup sliced almonds. Combine and press in a 2-quart bowl or mold. This will make about a 3/4-inch layer covering the inside surface of the bowl. Smooth with the back side of a wet spoon. Freeze hard.

Second layer: 1 quart good quality vanilla ice cream. Add a 3/4-inch layer of vanilla ice cream over the pistachio, smooth and freeze hard.

Third layer: 1 quart raspberry frozen yogurt. Smooth over vanilla layer. Freeze.

Fourth layer: Ganache Cream (recipe follows). Spoon on top of raspberry layer to fill cavity. Level the top. Freeze at least 2 hours, preferably longer. Let bombe mellow in refrigerator about 30 minutes before serving. Unmold and garnish with whipped cream and pistachios, if desired. Slice in wedges to serve.

>**Ganache Cream.** 1/2 cup heavy cream, 1 1/2 ounces unsweetened chocolate, 2 1/2 ounces semi-sweet chocolate, pinch salt, 1 teaspoon powdered instant coffee, expresso if available. Microwave 1/4 cup cream, chocolate, salt and coffee on 70% power for about 1-2 minutes, or until chocolate melts, stirring several times. Do not boil. Stir until very smooth. Cool to room temperature. Whip remaining 1/4 cup cream and gently fold into chocolate mixture. Chill. Ganache may also be used as a cake or cookie filling, or thinned with additional coffee and served as a sauce over ice cream.

Lemon Meringue Pie

Just like Grandmother's and well worth the effort.

1 3/4 cups sugar
1/2 cup cornstarch
1/4 teaspoon salt
1 1/2 cups water
3 eggs, separated
1/2 cup lemon juice
2 teaspoons lemon rind, grated
2 tablespoons butter
Baked pie crust or graham cracker crust

Reserve 6 tablespoons sugar for meringue. Mix together the remaining sugar, cornstarch, water and salt. Microwave on HIGH 4-6 minutes or until mixture is transparent, stirring after mixture cooks 2 minutes. Beat egg yolks and lemon juice together, adding 1/2 cup of the hot mixture. Mix well and add to hot cornstarch mixture. Cook 4-6 minutes on 70% power, stirring several times until thickened. Add rind and butter. Mix well. To prevent film from forming on filling, place plastic wrap directly on surface while it cools.

Prepare meringue by beating egg whites and 1/4 teaspoon salt until soft peaks form. Gradually add 6 tablespoons sugar, continuing to beat until stiff. Pile meringue on top of filling, spreading to edges to prevent shrinking. Microwave on HIGH 2-3 minutes. Meringue will be light and firm, but not brown. To brown the meringue, use the conventional oven.

Atlanta Style Cheese Cake

Fill the center with strawberries for a
very impressive dessert. Simply Scrumptious!

2 (8-ounce) packages cream cheese
1 pound creamed cottage cheese
1 1/2 cups sugar
4 eggs
3 tablespoons cornstarch
3 tablespoons flour
1/4 cup lemon juice, freshly squeezed
1 tablespoon grated lemon rind
1 teaspoon vanilla
1/3 cup butter, melted
1 cup sour cream

Oil a microwave-safe bundt cake pan and sprinkle with sugar to coat. Soften cream cheese for 2-3 minutes on 30% power. Place in large mixing bowl and beat cream cheese and cottage cheese at high speed until well blended. Gradually add sugar, then eggs, beating well after each addition. Add cornstarch, flour, lemon juice, rind, and vanilla. Add melted butter and sour cream. Beat only until smooth. Pour into bundt pan and microwave for 18 minutes on 50% power, and 3-6 minutes on HIGH. Let stand in pan for two hours. Then remove and let cool before placing in refrigerator. Chill at least 3 hours before serving. Garnish with fresh strawberries or other fruit. Freezes well.

Quick Fruit Cobbler
Terrific winter dessert!

1 stick butter
1 cup milk
1 cup flour, self-rising
1 cup sugar
4 cups fruit (sweetened to taste)

Microwave butter on HIGH 1 minute to melt in a 2-quart casserole. Add milk, flour and sugar and mix together. Pour fruit over batter; do not stir. Microwave on HIGH 10-15 minutes or until done. If you want to brown the crust, sprinkle with sugar and cinnamon and place under the conventional broiler a few minutes. Serve with whipped cream, ice cream or a rum or vanilla sauce.

BLACK CHERRY PUDDING. Make Quick Fruit Cobbler, substituting a 16-ounce can dark, sweet cherries, drained and chopped and 1 cup chopped pecans for the fruit.

Pineapple-Lemon Pie

Crust:
1 1/2 cups sifted flour
1/4 cup sugar
1 teaspoon grated lemon peel
3/4 cup butter
1/2 cup oats
2 egg yolks

Filling:
1 cup sugar
1/4 cup cornstarch
1/4 teaspoon salt
1 cup water
1 (8-ounce) can crushed pineapple
4 egg yolks, slightly beaten
1 teaspoon grated lemon peel
1/3 cup lemon juice
1 tablespoon butter
3 tablespoons kirsch or rum (optional)
1 cup whipping cream, whipped

Prepare crust: Sift flour and sugar. Add peel. Cut in butter until mixture resembles coarse crumbs. Stir in oats. Add egg yolks. Knead lightly. Microwave in a 9-inch pie plate on HIGH 5-7 minutes.

Filling: Combine sugar, cornstarch and salt. Stir in water and pineapple. Microwave on HIGH 6-8 minutes, or until thickened and clear, stirring several times. Add egg yolks, blending the hot mixture into the eggs first. Microwave on HIGH 1 minute. Stir in peel, juice, butter and Kirsch. Cool slightly and pour into pie shell. Garnish with whipped cream and lemon curls.

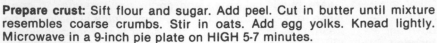

Chocolate Pecan Pie

Crust:

1 1/2 cups ground pecans
1 egg, separated
1/4 cup sugar
1 tablespoon cocoa

Filling:

6 ounces (1 cup) semi-sweet chocolate chips
1 egg, separated
1 teaspoon vanilla
1/2 pint heavy cream, whipped
1 tablespoon powdered sugar

Make crust: Beat egg white until stiff (reserve yolk for filling). Gradually add sugar, beating until stiff and glossy; beat in cocoa. Fold in ground nuts. Press mixture firmly onto bottom and sides of well buttered 9-inch pie plate. Microwave on HIGH 3-6 minutes.

Prepare filling: Melt chocolate on 70% power for 2-4 minutes. Stir in 2 egg yolks and vanilla; set aside to cool. Beat remaining egg white until stiff; set aside. Whip cream; add sugar. Fold half of cream into chocolate mixture. Then fold in beaten egg white. Pile into pie shell; garnish with remaining whipped cream and chocolate curls. Chill.

Rum Cream Pie
Simply Scrumptious! Good light Thanksgiving or Christmas dessert!

Crust:

2 1/4 cups graham cracker crumbs
1/2 cup butter, melted
2 tablespoons sugar
1/2 teaspoon ground cinnamon
1/2 cup chopped pecans

Filling:

1 envelope unflavored gelatin
1/2 cup cold water
5 egg yolks
1 cup sugar
1/3 cup Meyer's dark rum
1 1/2 cups whipping cream, whipped
Unsweetened chocolate, shaved for garnish

Combine crust ingredients and press in a 9-inch pie plate. Microwave on HIGH 3 minutes. Chill. Soften gelatin in water. Microwave on HIGH 45 seconds - 1 minute to dissolve gelatin. Beat egg yolks and sugar until very light. Stir gelatin into egg mixture. Cool. Gradually add rum, beating constantly. Fold whipped cream into egg mixture. Cool until mixture begins to set, then spoon into crust. Chill until firm. Top with grated chocolate.

Try substituting other liquors or liqueurs for the rum. For example: bourbon, praline liqueur, Kahlua, amaretto.

Steamed Prune Pudding
Delicious Christmas Tradition!

Steamed puddings microwave beautifully! The appearance is the same as conventionally baked. Microwave cooking time: about 15 minutes. Conventional cooking time: 2 hours.

Serves 8

1 1/4 cups sifted flour
1/2 teaspoon salt
1 teaspoon baking soda
5 tablespoons butter
1 1/4 cups firmly packed brown sugar
3 eggs
1 box pitted prunes
2 tablespoons milk
1/4 cup vegetable oil
Powdered sugar

Add 3/4 cup water to prunes, cover with plastic wrap and microwave on HIGH 5 minutes. Let prunes sit until plumped, then drain. Sift flour, salt and baking soda together. Beat butter, sugar, and eggs thoroughly, add prunes. Blend in dry ingredients. Add milk and oil. Avoid overmixing. Prepare a 6-cup ring mold or other heat proof ceramic mold by greasing well and dusting with graham cracker crumbs. Spread batter in mold, cover tightly with plastic wrap. Secure wrap around the dish with rubber band. Sit mold on an inverted pie plate in the oven; microwave on 50% power for 13 minutes and HIGH 2-8 minutes or until done. Cool covered on a heatproof surface 10 minutes. Invert; dust with powdered sugar. Serve with hard sauce or whipped cream.

Hard Sauce. 1/2 cup butter, 2 cups powdered sugar, 2 tablespoons brandy. Beat butter until fluffy. Mix in remaining ingredients.

Banana Pudding Cream Filling

1 1/2 cups milk or half-and-half
1 egg
2 tablespoons cornstarch
1/4 teaspoon salt
3/4 cup sugar
1 teaspoon vanilla
3 tablespoons butter

Microwave milk on HIGH for 3-5 minutes or to boiling. Mix sugar, cornstarch and egg together. Add about 1/2 cup of hot milk, stirring to blend. Add to remaining milk and cook for 4-5 minutes on 70% power or until thickened. Add butter, vanilla and salt. Cool.

To make banana pudding, layer vanilla wafers and banana slices. Pour half of cream filling over bananas and repeat layers.

Soften ice cream or melt a slice of cheese on apple pie in 15-20 seconds per piece on HIGH.

Judie's Japanese Fruit Pie

1 stick butter
3/4 cup sugar
3 eggs
1/2 cup coconut
1/2 cup pecans
1/2 cup chocolate chips
9-inch baked pie shell

Microwave butter and chocolate in a deep bowl on 70% power for about 2 minutes. Stir to melt. Stir in pecans, coconut, sugar and eggs. Pour filling into baked pastry shell and microwave on 50% power about 8 minutes. Stir once, very gently, during cooking. Cool before serving.

Kay's Kahlua Pie

Crust:

1/2 cup butter
1 (7-ounce) can coconut
2 tablespoons flour
1/2 cup chopped pecans

Filling:

1/2 gallon coffee ice cream
Kahlua liqueur
1 cup whipping cream, whipped

Microwave butter in a 9-inch pie plate on HIGH 1/2 - 1 minute to melt. Mix in other crust ingredients. Press against bottom and sides of plate. Microwave on HIGH 2-3 minutes. Cool. Fill pie shell with ice cream. Pour Kahlua over ice cream. Top with whipped cream.

Becky's Chocolate Pie

Serves 8

Oatmeal pie crust
1 cup sugar
3 egg yolks
3 tablespoons each: flour, cocoa and butter
1 teaspoon vanilla
1 (13 ounce) can evaporated milk

Combine sugar, cocoa, flour and milk. Microwave on HIGH 1 1/2 minutes. Beat egg yolks and add to mixture. Microwave on HIGH 3-6 minutes or until thickened. Stir in butter and vanilla. Pour into cooked crust. Chill and serve with whipped cream — a must!

Chocolate curls. Place unwrapped block of chocolate in microwave and heat 7-10 seconds. Scrape the curls off with a vegetable peeler.

Heavenly Chocolate Dessert
(We think this is what the Angels eat!)

*Make five different Simply Scrumptious desserts with one basic recipe.
Each variation is equally good. Try them all!*

Serves 15-20

First layer:

1 cup flour
3/4 - 1 cup chopped pecans
1 stick butter

Mix and press into 9 x 13 inch dish. Cook at 70% for 4-6 minutes. Cool.

Second layer:

8 ounces cream cheese
1 cup powdered sugar
1 - 1 1/2 cups whipped cream

Soften cream cheese on HIGH 45-60 seconds. Stir in powdered sugar. Fold
in whipped cream. Spread over crust. Refrigerate 15 minutes.

Third layer:

1 cup sugar
3 egg yolks
3 tablespoons each, flour, cocoa, and butter
1 teaspoon vanilla
1 cup evaporated milk

Combine and microwave on HIGH 4-6 minutes or until thickened. Cool and
spread over second layer.

Fourth layer:

Top with whipped cream and refrigerate. Garnish with chocolate curls. Cut
in squares to serve.

Variations of this dessert may be made by replacing the third layer with one
of the following:

HEAVENLY STRAWBERRY DESSERT: 2 (10-ounce) packages frozen strawberries, 6 tablespoons cornstarch, 2/3 cup sugar, 2/3 cup water. Microwave frozen berries on HIGH 3-5 minutes to defrost. Mix cornstarch and sugar. Add other ingredients and microwave on HIGH 4-6 minutes or until thickened. Cool. Garnish whipped cream with fresh berries. (Try other fruit fillings, too.)

HEAVENLY COCONUT DESSERT: 6-ounce package frozen coconut, 1 (5 5/8-ounce) package vanilla instant pudding, 2 cups milk, 1 cup sour cream. Mix pudding, milk and sour cream. Sprinkle half of the coconut over second layer. Then spread pudding mixture over coconut. Use remaining coconut to sprinkle over top of whipped cream as final garnish.

HEAVENLY LEMON DESSERT: 2 (3-ounce) packages instant lemon pudding mix, 3 cups milk, 2 tablespoons lemon juice, 1 tablespoon grated lemon rind. Mix together and pour over second layer. Garnish with grated lemon rind, if desired.

HEAVENLY BLUEBERRY DESSERT: 3 cups blueberries, 2/3 cup sugar, 1/2 cup water, 1/4 cup lemon juice, 1/4 cup cornstarch. Mix and microwave on HIGH 3-4 minutes or until thickened.

Simply Scrumptious Caramel Cream Pie

Graham cracker pie shell
1 (14 ounce) can condensed milk
2 tablespoons milk
1 (4 ounce) carton whipped topping
(For a pie that is not so sweet, use unsweetened whipped cream.)

Microwave condensed milk in a deep container on 40% power for 12-18 minutes, stirring several times, until the milk caramelizes (turns a caramel color). Stir in 2 tablespoons milk to thin; let completely cool. Fold in whipped cream or topping and pour into pie shell. Chill. Garnish with whipped cream and nuts if desired.

🍂 Quick Date Nut Cream Pie: Fold 2/3 cup chopped dates and 2/3 cup chopped nuts into Caramel Cream before pouring into pie shell.

Simply Scrumptious Strawberry Pie

Serves 8

5 cups fresh strawberries
1 cup sugar
3 tablespoons cornstarch
Several drops red food coloring
Baked pastry shell or crumb crust
Whipped cream

Puree 2 cups berries in blender. Combine sugar and cornstarch, stir into pureed berries. Microwave on HIGH 2-3 minutes or until it starts to boil. Stir occasionally. Cook on 70% power about 5 minutes or until sauce is smooth and thickened, stirring several times. Add food coloring. Cool. Arrange remaining 3 cups of berries in pastry. Spoon cooled sauce over fresh strawberries. Chill and garnish with whipped cream.

Sauces

Enjoy these sauces on ice cream, cream puffs, crepes, cakes, custards, cheese cake or fruits.

The microwave oven eliminates the possibility of scorching because the cooking occurs from all sides rather than only from the bottom. Continuous stirring is replaced with occasional stirring. Sauces made with cornstarch thicken more rapidly and need less stirring than those thickened with flour.

Sauces may be measured, mixed and cooked in the same dish. Use a deep bowl at least 2 to 3 times the volume of the sauce. (We recommend a 2-quart measuring cup.)

Chocolate Sauce: 12 ounces semi-sweet chocolate, 2 ounces unsweetened chocolate, 1/2 pint heavy cream, 2 tablespoons cognac or Grand Marnier. Microwave chocolate on 50% power 2 - 4 minutes to melt. Blend in other ingredients. Makes 1 1/4 cups of rich, delicious sauce for desserts.

Chocolate Sauce: 2 cups sugar, 1/4 cup cocoa, 1/4 cup butter, 1 (13 1/2-ounce) can evaporated milk, 2 teaspoons vanilla. Combine sugar, cocoa, butter and 1/2 cup milk and microwave on HIGH 3-5 minutes to dissolve sugar. Add remaining milk and cook on HIGH about 1 minute longer to slightly thicken. Add vanilla. Makes 3 cups.

Robyns' Caramel Nut Sauce: 1 1/2 cups sugar, 3/4 cup cream, 1 tablespoon butter, about 1/2 cup finely crushed nuts. Mix 1/2 cup sugar and 1 tablespoon water and microwave on HIGH about 4-7 minutes, stirring often until sugar turns light brown. Add remaining sugar and cream and microwave on HIGH until sugar has dissolved. Add butter and beat. Stir in nuts. Yield. 1 1/2 cups.

Strawberry Sauce: 1 (10-ounce) package frozen strawberries, 3 tablespoons cornstarch, 1/3 cup sugar, 1/4 cup water, 1 tablespoon lemon juice, few drops red food coloring (optional). Defrost berries by microwaving on HIGH 2 minutes. Combine cornstarch and juice. Stir in berries, microwave on HIGH 2-5 minutes or until thickened. Stir in lemon juice and coloring.

Bing-Cherry Sauce. Melt 3/4 cup currant jelly on HIGH about 1 minute. Stir in one (29 ounce) can pitted Bing cherries, drained. Microwave on HIGH until mixture boils.

Fresh Peach Sauce: 4 fresh peaches, peeled and mashed, 1/2 cup sugar, 1/2 cup orange juice, 2 teaspoons lemon juice, 1 teaspoon vanilla. Combine ingredients and microwave on HIGH until thickened.

Orange Sauce: 1/4 cup butter, 3 tablespoons sugar, 3 tablespoons Grand Marnier or Cointreau, 1 cup orange juice, 2 teaspoons cornstarch, 1/2 teaspoon grated lemon peel, 1/2 teaspoon grated orange peel. Combine butter and sugar, cook on HIGH about 2 minutes. Combine orange juice and cornstarch until smooth. Add to butter mixture. Add lemon and orange peel. Cover with plastic wrap and cook on HIGH 5 minutes. Add Grand Marnier. Yield 1 1/3 cups.

Sweet Cider Sauce: 2 tablespoons cornstarch, 2 cups sweet apple cider, 3 mashed allspice berries, 1 (1-inch) piece cinnamon stick, pinch of salt, dash nutmeg. Place cornstarch in 4 cup bowl. Gradually whisk in cider until mixture is smooth. Microwave, uncovered on HIGH 4 minutes. Whisk to blend. Stir in spices. Microwave on HIGH 1 - 1 1/2 minutes until thickened. Strain and serve warm with waffles, cake or gingerbread.

Vanilla Custard Sauce: 1/3 cup sugar, 4 egg yolks, 1/8 teaspoon salt, 2 cups half-and-half, 1 (1-inch piece) vanilla bean or 1/4 teaspoon vanilla extract. Beat sugar, egg yolks and salt until mixture thickens, 2-3 mintues. Microwave half-and-half with vanilla bean on HIGH 3-4 minutes just to boiling. Gradually pour hot milk mixture into egg yolk mixture, beating continuously. Microwave on 70% power until mixture thickens. Strain. Serve with fresh fruit or fruit desserts.

Blueberry Sauce: 3 cups blueberries, 2/3 cup sugar, 1/2 cup water, 1/4 cup lemon juice. Mix and microwave on HIGH 2-3 minutes.

Chocolate Syrup: (Use to make Chocolate Milk.) 1 1/2 cups sugar, 1 cup cocoa, dash salt, 1 cup hot water, 2 teaspoons vanilla. Mix sugar, cocoa, and salt in a deep bowl. Add 1/4 cup water, making a smooth paste. Add the remaining 3/4 cup water. Stir. Microwave on HIGH 1-2 minutes until mixture comes to a boil, stirring several times. Boil 3 minutes. Add vanilla, cool. Yields 2 cups.

Lemon Whipped Cream Sauce: 1 cup sugar, 1/2 cup lemon juice, 2 tablespoons grated lemon peel, 4 eggs, 1 cup whipping cream, whipped. Microwave sugar, lemon juice and peel on HIGH until sugar dissolves. Beat eggs. Add hot mixture to eggs while beating. Microwave on HIGH until mixture Is thickened, stirring several times. Cool thoroughly. Fold in whipped cream. Chill and serve over pound cake or fresh fruit.

Sabayon: 4 egg yolks, 1/4 cup sugar, 1/4 cup dry white wine, 1 tablespoon framboise, (raspberry brandy). Beat egg yolks and sugar until light and lemon colored. Gradually beat in wine and brandy. Microwave on 70% power 1-3 minutes until mixture thickens into fluffy custard. (Watch carefully and stop cooking before egg yolks curdle.)

Brandied Butterscotch Sauce: 3/4 cup dark brown sugar, dash salt, 1/2 cup water, 1 tablespoon instant coffee, 1/4 cup brandy, 1 (14-ounce) can sweetened condensed milk, 1 teaspoon vanilla. Combine sugar, salt and water and microwave on HIGH to soft-ball stage 230°F. Dissolve coffee in brandy. Add hot syrup to milk. Blend In brandy mixture and vanilla. Stir. Yields 2 cups.

Sour Cream Sauce: 1/2 cup brown sugar, 1/2 cup sour cream. Microwave on 50% power 1-2 minutes until sugar melts.

Maple Walnut Sauce: 1 1/2 cups maple syrup, 1 cup coarsely chopped walnuts, toasted. Microwave syrup until it boils and stir in walnuts. Serve hot or at room temperature. (Substitute corn syrup and other nuts for a nut sauce for ice cream.)

Cinnamon Syrup: 3/4 cup brown sugar, 1/4 teaspoon cinnamon, 1/4 cup butter, 1/2 cup water, 3 tablespoons light corn syrup. Microwave on HIGH until mixture thickens or reaches 225° F. Serve over waffles, ice cream or fruit desserts.

Zabaglione: 4 egg yolks, 1 whole egg, 1/4 cup sugar, dash salt, 1/2 cup marsala wine or sherry. Beat egg yolks, egg, sugar, and salt until thick and fluffy. Microwave marsala on HIGH 45 seconds or until warm. Gradually beat into egg mixture. Microwave on 50% power for several minutes stirring often or until mixture is double in volume and slightly thickened. Serve warm or cold with fresh fruit or cookies.

🐟 Enjoy hot toppings. Microwave an 11-ounce jar (lid removed) on HIGH for 30-45 seconds, stirring several times.

Scrumptious Apple Pie
The crust makes this pie extra good and quick!

4-5 cups peeled, sliced apples
1 tablespoon lemon juice
3/4 cup sugar
1/4 cup butter
Oatmeal pie crust with 1/2 teaspoon cinnamon added
    to ingredients (Pie crust recipe on page 158)

Place apples in a 2-quart bowl and sprinkle with lemon juice. Cover tightly with plastic wrap and microwave on HIGH for 5-7 minutes. Melt butter on HIGH 30 seconds and add sugar stirring to blend. Cook 1 additional minute and add to apples, tossing to coat. Cool slightly and pour in cooled pie crust. Serve warm with whipped cream, ice cream or a slice of cheese.

Austrian Chocolate Mousse

Yield: 6 servings

1 cup semi-sweet chocolate chips
1 ounce unsweetened chocolate
2 teaspoons vanilla
3/4 cup powdered sugar
1/2 cup butter, softened
4 eggs, separated
1 teaspoon instant coffee

Place chocolate chips and unsweetened chocolate in a deep bowl. Microwave on 70% power 2-4 minutes just until melted. Cool to lukewarm.

Place softened butter, powdered sugar, egg yolks, and instant coffee in food processor or mixing bowl and mix thoroughly. Add cooled chocolate, blending well.

Beat egg whites until stiff but not dry. Carefully fold whites into chocolate mixture. Pour into crystal bowl or sherbet glasses. Top with whipped cream to serve.

CHERRIES JUBILEE. 2/3 cup sugar, 2 tablespoons cornstarch, 1/8 teaspoon salt, 1/2 cup sweet red wine, 1 (22-ounce) can Bing Cherries, 1/3 cup cognac. Combine sugar, cornstarch and salt. Stir in 1/2 cup water and wine. Add cherries, cover with plastic wrap and microwave on HIGH until sauce is thickened, 3-5 minutes. Add cognac. To flame sauce, heat cognac in microwave on HIGH 30-40 seconds or until warm. Gently pour over cherries and ignite. When flame goes out, ladle cherries over ice cream and serve immediately.

Marinate bite-size chunks of fresh pineapple in crème de menthe. Spoon over fresh coconut ice cream. Garnish with sugared mint leaves.

A stabilizer in pudding mixes keeps them smooth and creamy, even when cooked on HIGH.

Simply Scrumptious
Cookies & Candies

Cookies & Candies

Cookies

Candies

Cookies - General Guidelines

Bar cookies exemplify the best of microwaving. Their taste, texture and appearance compare favorably with conventional baking and they can be ready to serve in 6-10 minutes (less time than it takes to pre-heat the conventional oven).

Use a square dish and shield the corners with foil. There is no need to grease the dish. After baking, let stand directly on the countertop 5-10 minutes to complete cooking. Cover dish with waxed paper.

Individual cookies must be microwaved 6-10 at a time; therefore, it is usually more efficient to bake large batches conventionally. Microwaved cookies are soft and chewy. It is difficult to make a crisp cookie. To keep dough from spreading thin and becoming too tender, the dough must be stiffer than a conventional recipe, almost crumbly. Frosting, confectioners sugar or crumbs add eye appeal since the cookies don't brown. To microwave, place cookies on waxed paper on a dish 2 inches apart in a circular pattern. Microwave most cookies at 50% power. Over-baked cookies will burn in the middle.

Oatmeal Cookie Squares

Yield 16-24 cookies

1/2 cup butter
1/2 cup brown sugar, firmly packed
1 egg
1 teaspoon vanilla
1 teaspoon baking powder
1 1/2 cups quick-cooking oats
3/4 cup flour
1/2 cup chopped nuts
1/2 cup raisins or chocolate chips

Cream butter, sugar and vanilla. Add egg and beat. Add remaining ingredients. Press mixture into 8-inch square dish. Cover with plastic wrap and microwave on 70% power for 4-6 minutes; uncover and cook on HIGH 1-2 minutes. Cool and cut into squares.

> **Oatmeal Scotchies:** Instead of chocolate chips, fold in butterscotch chips.

> **Children's Favorite:** Instead of chocolate chips, immediately after cooking, lightly press M&M's in the top of the cookies.

> **Oatmeal Carrot Cookies:** Reduce the oatmeal from 1 1/2 cups to 3/4 cup and add 1/2 cup grated carrots, 1 teaspoon cinnamon and 1/4 teaspoon nutmeg.

Delicious Coconut Bars

Crust:

6 tablespoons butter
1/4 cup dark brown sugar
1 cup flour
1/2 cup finely chopped pecans

Filling:

2 eggs
1 cup sugar
1/2 teaspoon vanilla
1/2 teaspoon baking powder
1 1/2 cups coconut (toasted is better)

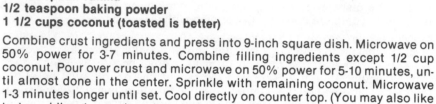

Combine crust ingredients and press into 9-inch square dish. Microwave on 50% power for 3-7 minutes. Combine filling ingredients except 1/2 cup coconut. Pour over crust and microwave on 50% power for 5-10 minutes, until almost done in the center. Sprinkle with remaining coconut. Microwave 1-3 minutes longer until set. Cool directly on counter top. (You may also like to try adding 1 cup chocolate chips to the coconut filling.)

Variations: Make other bar cookies using the "Delicious" crust.

Delicious Date Bars: Use Date nut filling on page 179. Spread on baked "Delicious" crust and microwave on HIGH 4-8 minutes until set. Sprinkle powdered sugar on top.

Cheese Cake Delights: 8-ounces cream cheese, 1/2 cup sugar, 1 egg, 1 tablespoon orange juice concentrate, 1 teaspoon grated orange peel, 1 tablespoon milk. Microwave cream cheese on 50% power about 45 seconds to soften. Add remaining ingredients. Spread on crust. Cover with plastic wrap and cook on 70% power for 5-6 minutes or until set about 1 inch from center. Sprinkle with powdered sugar.

Lemon Bars

Crust:

1/2 cup butter
1 cup flour
1/4 cup powdered sugar

Filling:

3 eggs
2 tablespoons lemon juice
1 teaspoon lemon rind
1/2 teaspoon baking powder
1 cup sugar
2 tablespoons flour
Powdered sugar

Combine crust ingredients and cut into fine crumbs with food processor or fork. Press in bottom of 9-inch square pan. Microwave on HIGH 3-4 minutes or until surface looks dull. Mix all ingredients for filling and pour over baked crust. Cover with plastic film and microwave on 70% power for 5-7 minutes or until set about 1 inch from the center. Cool covered on counter top. Sprinkle the top lightly with powdered sugar and cut in bars.

Peanut Butter Bars

1/2 cup butter
1 cup dark brown sugar
1/2 cup crunchy peanut butter
2 eggs
1 cup flour
1 teaspoon baking powder
1/4 teaspoon salt
6 ounces chocolate chips (optional)

Heat butter on HIGH for 30 seconds to melt. Add sugar, peanut butter and eggs. Combine flour, baking powder and salt. Add to peanut butter mixture. Stir in chocolate chips. Pour into 9-inch square dish. Microwave on HIGH power for 5-7 minutes. Let stand on counter top to cool. When cool, cut into bars.

Chocolate Chip Pan Cookies

Yield 24 bars

1/2 cup butter
3/4 cup dark brown sugar
1 egg
1 tablespoon milk
1 teaspoon vanilla
1 cup flour
1/2 teaspoon baking powder
Dash of salt
1 cup semisweet chocolate pieces
1/2 cup nuts

Cream butter and sugar. Add egg, vanilla and milk. Mix well. Combine flour, baking powder and salt. Add to creamed mixture. Blend and stir in 1/2 cup chocolate pieces and 1/4 cup nuts. Spread in 9-inch square dish. Sprinkle remaining 1/2 cup chocolate pieces and 1/4 cup nuts on top. Microwave on HIGH 4-7 minutes. Cool and cut into bars.

Kwick Krackle Cookies

1 (18 1/2-ounce) box devil's food cake mix
2 eggs
1/3 cup solid vegetable shortening
1/2 cup chopped nuts, optional
Powdered sugar

Combine ingredients (except powdered sugar) in bowl with fork. Shape in balls no larger than 1 inch. Chill thoroughly. Place in freezer about 15 minutes or refrigerator for several hours. Roll in powdered sugar. (Sugar adheres more to the cold dough.) Place 6-8 balls in a circle on waxed paper on a baking dish. Place one in the center. Cook on 50% power for 1 1/4 - 2 minutes or just until surface is dry. Remove to rack or towel to cool.

Great when children want to make cookies and mommy doesn't. Children love to watch them "crackle" in the microwave oven. You may want to refrigerate the balls covered for several days so the children can enjoy watching them cook many times.

Scratch Brownies
Fudgy!

1/2 cup butter
6 tablespoons cocoa
1 cup granulated or brown sugar
1 egg (2 eggs for a cake-type brownie)
1 teaspoon vanilla
3/4 cup flour
1/2 teaspoon baking powder
1/4 teaspoon salt
1/2 cup chopped nuts

Melt butter and cocoa together. Microwave on HIGH 1 - 1 1/2 minutes. Add sugar, then other ingredients. Microwave on HIGH 5 1/2 - 6 minutes. Good as a bar cookie or topped with ice cream and chocolate sauce for a quick dessert.

Blonde Brownies: Omit cocoa and use brown sugar instead of white. You may stir in 1/2 cup chocolate chips.

Peanut Butter Frosted Brownies: Cook blonde brownies. Immediately after taking out of the oven, sprinkle them with 1/2 cup chocolate chips and spoons of peanut butter (about 1/4 cup). When soft, spread and swirl for marbled effect.

Butterscotch Brownies: Make Scratch Brownie recipe using brown sugar instead of white and omit the cocoa. Fold in 6 ounces of butterscotch chips.

Kathy's Cheesecake Bars

Yield 30-40 bars

6 tablespoons butter
1/3 cup dark brown sugar, firmly packed
1 cup sifted flour
1/4 cup chopped pecans
1/4 cup sugar
1 (8-ounce) package cream cheese
1 egg, beaten
1 tablespoon milk
1 tablespoon lemon juice
1/2 teaspoon vanilla

Cream butter and brown sugar; add flour and chopped pecans. Cream with spoon until mixture forms crumbs. Set aside 1 cup of mixture for topping. Press remaining mixture into 8-inch square dish. Bake on HIGH 3 - 3 1/2 minutes. Combine white sugar and cream cheese. Beat until smooth. Add egg, milk, lemon juice and vanilla. Beat. Spread over baked crumbs. Sprinkle reserved crumbs over top. Cover with plastic wrap and cook on 50% power for 5 minutes. Uncover and cook on HIGH 1-2 minutes. Cut into bars and store in refrigerator. Delicious!

☞ Commercial brownie mix. Combine ingredients according to package directions and microwave on HIGH 7-9 minutes (8-inch dish).

Filled Oatmeal Bars

Base:
1/2 cup butter
1/2 cup brown sugar
1/4 teaspoon salt
1 cup quick cooking oats
1 cup flour

Mix butter, sugar and salt. Add oats and flour. Mix to form crumbs. Reserve 1 cup. Press remaining mixture in an 8-inch square dish. Microwave 3-7 minutes on 50% power or just until dull-looking. Spread one of the following fillings over crust. Sprinkle with reserved crumbs and microwave on HIGH 4-8 minutes.

Raspberry: 3/4 cup raspberry jam. (Any flavor jam may be used.)

Mincemeat: 1 cup prepared mincemeat.

Date Nut: 1 cup dates, 1/3 cup water, 3 tablespoons sugar, 1 tablespoon lemon juice, 1/2 cup finely chopped walnuts. Combine ingredients, except walnuts, and microwave on HIGH 3-5 minutes, or until thick and smooth, stirring several times. Add nuts.

Chocolate: 1 cup sweetened condensed milk, 1 cup semisweet chocolate chips, 1/2 cup nuts, optional. Cook milk on HIGH 1 minute. Stir in chips and nuts. Stir to melt chocolate. Microwave an additional 30 seconds if needed.

Butterscotch: Same as for chocolate, but use butterscotch chips.

Caramel: 1 can sweetened condensed milk, 2 tablespoons milk, 1/2 cup nuts, optional. Cook condensed milk on 40% power for 12-15 minutes, stirring occasionally, until milk is caramel colored and thick. Fold in 2 tablespoons milk and nuts.

Lemon Cheese: 8-ounces cream cheese, 1/3 cup sugar, 1 egg, 1 tablespoon lemon juice, 1 teaspoon grated lemon peel, 2 tablespoons milk. Soften cream cheese by microwaving on HIGH about 45 seconds. Add remaining ingredients.

Prune: 1 cup pitted prunes, 1/3 cup water, 1/2 cup brown sugar, 1 tablespoon lemon juice, 1/8 teaspoon salt, 1/3 cup chopped walnuts (optional). Combine and microwave on HIGH 3-5 minutes, stirring several times. Purée in blender. You may want to add 1/2 teaspoon ground cinnamon to the base mixture.

🍥 Use flavored sugars to garnish cookies. To flavor sugar, drop a vanilla bean, slightly dried lemon peel or orange peel into a small cannister of sugar. Keep closed several days or longer.

🍥 When baking cookies conventionally, test a few in the microwave. You'll soon learn which ones are suitable for microwaving.

🍥 To soften brown sugar, add a few drops of water or a slice of apple to the box and microwave on HIGH 15 seconds.

Crème De Menthe Squares

Yield 40-45 pieces

Crust:
1/3 cup butter
1/3 cup cocoa
1 1/2 cups graham cracker crumbs
1/3 cup powdered sugar
1 egg
1 teaspoon vanilla

Filling:
1/3 cup butter
1/4 cup Crème De Menthe (green)
2 1/2 cups powdered sugar

Topping:
1/4 cup butter
1 1/2 cups chocolate chips

Melt butter for crust by microwaving on HIGH. Add cocoa, then other ingredients. Press into 8-inch square dish and microwave 1 1/2 - 3 1/2 minutes on 50% power.

Melt butter for filling. Add Crème de Menthe and sugar. Spread over chocolate layer and chill.

Make topping by melting together butter and chocolate chips on 70% power for 2-3 minutes. Stir and pour over green layer. Chill and cut in small squares. Very rich!

Crème de Almond Squares: Substitute Crème de Almond (red) or other almond liqueur for crème de menthe. If liqueur is clear in color, a few drops of red food coloring may be added to make a pink filling. You may garnish with a slice of almond on top of the chocolate.

 Pink almond and green mint fillings are especially pretty at Christmas.

Sherry Cream Dreams: Substitute 2 tablespoons sherry, 2 tablespoons milk, and 1/2 cup chopped walnuts for the crème de menthe.

Date Balls

1 1/2 sticks butter
1 box chopped, pitted dates
3/4 cup sugar
1/2 cup chopped nuts or 1/2 cup coconut
2 cups Rice Krispies
Powdered sugar

Combine butter, sugar and dates. Microwave on HIGH 3 1/2 - 6 minutes or until thickened. Cool slightly. Add nuts or coconut and Rice Krispies. Roll into balls about 1 inch in diameter. Roll in powdered sugar.

Candies - General Guidelines

Both old fashioned cooked candies and short-cut candies microwave easily. Candy will not scorch since there is no direct heat. It needs stirring only a couple of times during cooking to equalize heat. Usually 70% power is best to keep candy from boiling over. Sugar becomes very hot when boiled. Use a container that can withstand high temperatures and is 2 to 3 times the volume of the candy ingredients. A 2-quart measuring cup is ideal since it is heat tempered, deep and has a handle.

A conventional mercury thermometer cannot be used in the microwave oven when the oven is operating; it will be damaged and will not register accurately. Check the syrup temperature with the thermometer as soon as the oven door is opened to get an accurate reading. You may prefer the cold water tests to determine doneness. COLD WATER TESTS: Fill a cup with cold water; drop about 1/2 teaspoon of boiling candy syrup into the cold water. Pick up the ball to judge its consistency and stage of doneness.

Candy	Test in Cold Water	Degrees on Candy Thermometer at Sea Level
Fudge Fondant	Soft ball (can be picked up but flattens)	234° F - 240° F
Caramels	Firm Ball (holds shape unless pressed)	242° F - 248° F
Divinity Taffy Caramel Corn	Hard Ball (Holds shape though pliable)	250° F - 268° F
Butterscotch English toffee	Soft Crack (separates into hard threads but not brittle)	270° F - 290° F
Brittles	Hard Crack (separates into hard and brittle threads)	300° F - 310° F

Dipped Peanut Butter Sandwich

Town House crackers
Creamy peanut butter
White chocolate coating

Spread peanut butter between 2 crackers making a "sandwich". Dip in melted white chocolate. (See information about dipping chocolates in Candy chapter.) Place on wax paper to dry. Semisweet dark chocolate is also good.

Simply Scrumptious Butterscotch Fudge

This is a truly creamy, delicious fudge! An old fashioned fudge with modern convenience. Be sure to try each variation. By altering the ingredients you can make several scrumptious flavors.

Yield: 48 pieces

1/4 cup butter
1 cup brown sugar
1 cup sugar
3/4 cup sour cream
1 teaspoon vanilla
1/2 cup chopped walnuts

Microwave butter in a deep bowl on HIGH about 1 minute or until melted. Add brown sugar and heat to boiling by microwaving on 50%-70% power for 3 to 4 minutes. Add sugar and sour cream. Microwave on 50-70% power for 15-20 minutes to soft ball stage, 236° F. Without stirring, cool at room temperature to lukewarm. Beat with the electric mixer until mixture holds its shape and loses its gloss. Quickly add vanilla and nuts. Spread immediately in a buttered 8-inch square pan. Cool and cut into squares. Garnish with additional nuts if desired.

Simply Scrumptious Vanilla Fudge: Make "Butterscotch Fudge" using 2 cups granulated sugar and no brown sugar.

Simply Scrumptious Chocolate Fudge: Make "Butterscotch Fudge" following the recipe exactly, but adding 3 to 4 squares unsweetened chocolate with the sour cream.

🐷 This fudge is delicious to use as centers for dipped chocolates. Just form the fudge into balls or desired shapes, chill thoroughly and dip in chocolate.

Uncooked Fudge

1 pound powdered sugar, sifted
1 stick butter
1/3 cup cocoa
1/4 cup milk
1 teaspoon vanilla

Microwave butter, cocoa and sugar on HIGH 2 minutes, stirring a time or two as butter melts. Add milk and vanilla. Microwave on HIGH 1 minute longer. Pour into an 8-inch square dish and freeze 1/2 hour.

🐷 "Uncooked" candies have a better flavor if microwaved for a minute or two.

🐷 **Chocolate Leaves:** Wash a rose leaf. Melt chocolate chips. Pull a single leaf upside down over surface of melted chocolate. Remove extra chocolate by shaking leaf slightly and tapping against side of the bowl. Place leaf, chocolate side up on cookie sheet to harden. (Make a curved leaf by letting it dry over curved surface such as cardboard roll.) Then peel off leaf. Veins of the real leaf will be imprinted in the chocolate. An elegant dessert garnish. May also use butterscotch chips instead of chocolate.

Fast Scotch Fudge

12 ounces butterscotch pieces
1 (14-ounce) can sweetened condensed milk
1 (12-ounce) jar creamy peanut butter

Microwave butterscotch pieces on HIGH 2-3 minutes until melted. Stir in other ingredients and cook on HIGH 1-2 minutes longer until bubbly. Pour in buttered 8-inch square dish. Refrigerate until set. Cut in squares.

Fast Rum Fudge

18 ounces semisweet chocolate chips
1 (14-ounce) can sweetened condensed milk
1/4 teaspoon salt
2 cups chopped walnuts
2 tablespoons Meyer's dark rum

Melt chocolate chips in mixing bowl. Microwave 2-3 minutes on 70% power or until melted, stirring several times. Add milk and salt, beat until smooth. Stir in rum and nuts. Spread evenly in an 8-inch dish and refrigerate until hardened.

Fast Chocolate Fudge

Yield: 36 pieces

2 1/2 - 3 cups semisweet chocolate chips
1 (14-ounce) can sweetened condensed milk
1/4 cup butter
1 cup chopped pecans

Microwave chips, milk and butter on 50% - 70% power until chocolate melts, 3-5 minutes, stirring several times. Add nuts and pour into a well buttered 8-inch square baking dish. Refrigerate until set.

Peppermint Fudge. Omit nuts and add 1/8 teaspoon peppermint oil.

Fast Vanilla Fudge

12 ounces white chocolate
1 (14-ounce) can condensed milk
1/4 cup butter

Microwave chips, milk and butter on 50% power until chocolate melts, 3-5 minutes, stirring several times. Pour into well buttered 8-inch square dish. Chill until firm and cut in 1-inch squares. Store in covered containers.

Variations: After cooking, stir in one of the following additions:
1 cup almonds and 1 teaspoon almond extract
1 cup chopped dates and 1 cup chopped walnuts
1/4 cup chopped black walnuts
1 cup candied fruit

"Fast Fudge" has a texture of caramels. For a texture change, beat the mixture on high speed with an electric mixer after all ingredients have been added, except nuts and fruits, for 3-5 minutes. Chill 5 minutes and beat again to achieve a lighter, creamier texture.

Toffee

Makes 1 pound

1 cup butter
1 1/3 cups sugar
1 tablespoon light corn syrup
2 tablespoons water
1 1/2 teaspoons vanilla
1/2 cup chocolate chips
1/2 cup finely chopped pecans

Combine butter, sugar, syrup and water in a deep bowl and microwave on 70% power 15-20 minutes or to hard crack stage (300° F). Stir in vanilla. Pour into buttered 13 x 9-inch pan. Sprinkle with chocolate chips. After 2 minutes spread them over the toffee. Sprinkle with nuts and lightly press into chocolate. Chill. Break into pieces.

Bark Candy

Bark Candy is a good way to use bits of leftover dipping chocolate. Pour melted chocolate coating or real chocolate (tempered for best results) over toasted nuts. Cool and break into serving-size pieces.

Almond Bark: Makes 1 1/2 pounds. 1 cup almonds, 1 pound white chocolate. Toast almonds by spreading them in a single layer in a pie plate and microwaving on HIGH 4-7 minutes until toasted. Let stand about 2 minutes. Melt chocolate by microwaving on 50% power until softened, 2-3 minutes. Stir in almonds and spread on baking sheet and refrigerate. Break into pieces.

Variations: Other Bark combinations may be made by using other flavor coatings such as chocolate, butterscotch or caramel; and other nuts such as walnuts, peanuts, pecans, coconut or dates, raisins or mixed nuts, or candied fruit bits.

Marbled Bark Candy: Makes 2 pounds. 2 pounds white chocolate coating, 2 tablespoons butter, 3 or 4 drops oil flavoring (peppermint, orange, spearmint, etc.). Coloring, use paste coloring or tinted chocolate. Place 1 pound chocolate coating and 1 tablespoon butter in a dish to melt. Place the other pound chocolate coating and 1 tablespoon butter, flavoring and coloring in another dish to melt. Melt the colored, flavored mixture by microwaving on 50% power for 2-3 mintues. Stir to combine. When smooth, spread thinly on waxed paper. Immediately microwave the white chocolate on 50% power for 2-3 minutes to melt. Stir until smooth; dribble over the tinted chocolate in a swirled pattern. With a knife or spatula, cut through both colors, marbilizing the chocolates. Let candy harden and break in pieces.

Try using milk chocolate or dark chocolate marbled with another color; for example, dark chocolate and green mint flavored white chocolate.

Combine 1 pound chocolate, 1 1/4 cups roasted peanuts and 2 1/2 cups pretzels.

Microwave candy thermometers are available. They register up to 320°F. and can be used in the oven during microwaving.

Almond Chocolate Cream Centers
Simply Scrumptious!

Makes 4-5 dozen

1 cup whipping cream
10 ounces semi-sweet chocolate, finely chopped
3 tablespoons butter
1/4 cup coarsely chopped toasted almonds
1/4 cup amaretto
1/8 teaspoon almond extract
1 - 1 1/2 pounds semi-sweet chocolate

Microwave cream on HIGH 1-2 minutes to simmering. Add chocolate and butter. Whisk until smooth. Cool to lukewarm. Stir in almonds, amaretto and extract. Cover and refrigerate until firm, 4 hours or overnight. Make 1-inch balls. Freeze uncovered until hard. Dip in chocolate.

Brazil Nut Creams. Substitute toasted brazil nuts for almonds, and white chocolate for semi-sweet chocolate. Before coating sets, lightly sift cocoa over dipped truffles.

Kirsch Chocolate Creams. Substitute 3 tablespoons kirsch for amaretto and extract.

 Make candy patties instead of balls and dip in chocolate.

Caramel Centers. Microwave 1 can condensed milk in a deep bowl at 40% power about 12-15 minutes until it caramelizes. Stir several times during cooking. Stir in 4 tablespoons milk. Cool and shape into balls. (Add 1/2 cup nuts if desired). Refrigerate several hours and dip in chocolate.

Black Wanut Divinity

Makes about 30 pieces

2 cups granulated sugar
1/2 cup cold water
1 teaspoon vinegar
1 egg white
1/2 teaspoon vanilla
1/4 cup chopped black walnuts

Combine sugar, water and vinegar in a deep bowl. Microwave covered on 70% power for 12-15 minutes or until candy reaches 240° F (firm ball). Meanwhile, beat egg white until stiff peaks form. Pour syrup in a thin stream into the egg white, while beating constantly with electric mixer. Add vanilla; beat until stiff. Fold in nuts. Drop by teaspoonfuls onto wax paper; cool.

Variations of Divinity may be made by making the following substitutions.

Maple Nut Divinity: Use 1 cup white sugar and 1 cup brown sugar. Substitute maple flavoring for vanilla and 1/2 cup chopped pecans for black walnuts.

Holiday Divinity: Instead of black walnuts, use 1/2 cup chopped walnuts and 1/4 cup chopped candied cherries. Add food colorings as desired to make pastel colors.

Simply Scrumptious Chocolates!
Truffles, bonbons, and other delights!

When cooking with chocolate, the biggest advantage of the microwave oven is the absence of direct heat. If chocolate is overcooked, it will become bitter and grainy. Microwave on 70% power to heat chocolate gently. Breaking chocolate into smaller pieces promotes even and faster melting. (Food processors are great!) Chocolate chips work well, too.

Never cover when melting chocolate. Steam will condense on the bottom of the lid; water in chocolate will cause it to thicken and loose its shine. Never add water, milk or other liquids directly to chocolate. Use oil flavorings, never alcohol or water base. White chocolate may be colored by using a paste or powdered coloring, not liquid food coloring.

When microwaving chocolate, the chocolate will retain its shape, but the appearance will change from dull to shiny. The chocolate will be softened, and stirring will mix the melted chocolate so that it is liquid and smooth. When it will not melt properly, it is probably old or has absorbed moisture. Stir about a tablespoon of coconut oil, paramount crystals or vegetable oil in to assist melting.

Store chocolate tightly wrapped since it readily absorbs odors. Never store in the freezer or refrigerator, it may become damp and not melt. Store in a plastic bag in a cool dry place. If it is stored for a long time, it may become dry, but it is still usable. Add a little vegetable oil.

The quality of chocolate varies with manufacturers. Select a good quality. Poor quality chocolate will make waxy, poor quality candy. The difference between real chocolate and chocolate flavored coatings is the oil base used in the product. Real chocolate is better quality, more expensive and requires more skill. Beginners may choose to use a coating, then move to real chocolate since chocolate coating is easier to work with.

Tempering. (The temperature probe is very helpful.) It is not necessary to temper chocolate coatings, but real chocolate must be tempered before using. If it is not, the finished product will have white streaks, be dull, and take a long time to set up. Tempering is simply heating dark chocolate to 100° F or white chocolate to 92°F., cooling it, then heating back up to the desired temperature. This results in a shiny candy. After tempering the chocolate, dip one center (pretzel, nut, etc.). It should set in a few mintues. If it has not set in 10 minutes, repeat the tempering process. The temperature probe is helpful to determine when you have reached the dipping temperature without overheating.

Temperature for dipping: Real chocolate — milk — 86° F
— dark — 90° F
Chocolate flavored coatings — 98° F

If chocolate is too thick, microwave several seconds longer. If too thin, cool. Keep chocolate stirred while dipping.

We prefer pure chocolate. Never add paraffin.

The secret to successful candy making is that the sugar must be dissolved slowly. Microwave at a reduced power level of 70% or lower for best results and to prevent sugaring.

Swiss Chocolate Gnache

1 1/2 cups whipping cream
8 ounces semi-sweet chocolate, finely chopped

Microwave cream on HIGH 1-2 minutes to simmering. Add chocolate and whip till thick. Consistency should be that of whipped cream. Cool, refrigerate 4 hours or overnight until firm. Make 1-inch balls. Freeze centers uncovered 4 hours. Dip in chocolate.

These centers are soft to handle. That's why freezing is needed before dipping. However the results are worth the effort. The finished candies yield a creamy delicious center.

Grand Mariner Gnache. Add 3 tablespoons Grand Marnier to cooled Gnache. After dipped, garnish top of bonbons with small pieces of candied orange peel if desired.

Mocha Gnache. Add 3 tablespoons instant coffee and finely chopped nuts (optional) to cooled Gnache.

Cordial Creams. Add 3 tablespoons Irish Whiskey or any preferred liqueur to cooled Gnache. Cherry liqueur is delicious! Try créme de menthe, too.

Chocolate Cups: Serve a light mousse or fruit in chocolate cups for an elegant dessert. Melt semi-sweet chocolate chips. Drizzle a heaping teaspoonful at a time down sides of fluted paper or foil baking cup to cover sides evenly. About 3 teaspoons will cover inside of cup. Repeat with remaining cups. Set cups in muffin pan. Refrigerate about 30 minutes until chocolate is firm. About 30 minutes before serving, with cool hands, gently peel paper from chocolate cups. Set on chilled platter and refrigerate until ready to use.

Chocolate Coffee Truffles
A very rich creamy center!

Makes 3-4 dozen

8 ounces semi-sweet chocolate
3 egg yolks
1/3 cup coffee liqueur
1/2 cup butter

Melt chocolate on 50% power for 3-4 minutes. Stir until smooth. Beat in egg yolks one at a time. Blend in liqueur. Microwave on 70% power for 1 minute. Add softened butter 1 tablespoon at a time while beating. Continue beating 4-5 minutes. Freeze several hours. Form into 1-inch balls. Return to freezer several hours to thoroughly chill. Dip in chocolate.

Graham Cracker Delights
Simply Scrumptious peanut butter centers!

2 cups crushed graham crackers
1 cup coconut
1 cup chopped pecans
1 cup peanut butter
1 box powdered sugar
1 tablespoon vanilla
2 sticks melted butter

Mix all ingredients. Roll into 1-inch balls. Dip in melting chocolate.

Delicious Bonbon Centers

Coconut Bonbons. In a deep bowl, microwave 1/2 cup white corn syrup on HIGH for 1-2 minutes or to rolling boil. Add small package of coconut. Mix thoroughly. Cool. Roll mixture into 1-inch balls. Chill and dip in chocolate.

Easy Homemade Fondant. Gradually add 4 cups powdered sugar to 2/3 cup condensed milk. Add 1/4 teaspoon salt and 1 1/2 teaspoons vanilla. Sprinkle confectioners sugar on a board and knead fondant until smooth and creamy. Wrap in plastic wrap and place in refrigerator to ripen for 24 hours. Can be flavored and used as cream centers.

Chocolate Covered Cherries. Wrap EASY HOMEMADE FONDANT around a maraschino cherry and dip in chocolate. For an especially good chocolate covered cherry, wrap the cherry with WHITE FUDGE that has been kneaded until pliable.

Peanut Cream Centers. 1/4 cup powdered sugar, 1/2 cup condensed milk, 1 cup creamy peanut butter, 6 ounces semi-sweet chocolate chips, 7 tablespoons chocolate flavored decorator candies. Combine sugar, milk and peanut butter in a medium mixing bowl. Stir until well blended. Stir in chocolate and chill until firm. Shape into small balls and roll each in chocolate decorator candies. Refrigerate until firm. Makes 6 dozen.

Butterscotch Creams. 1 cup butterscotch chips, 8-ounces cream cheese, 1 3/4 cups powdered sugar. Microwave chips on 70% power 2-3 minutes. Add cream cheese, then sugar. Spread in buttered dish and chill. Remove from refrigerator and form into 1-inch balls. Freeze, dip in chocolate. Garnish while still moist with finely grated nuts or graham cracker crumbs.

Crunchy Peanut Butter Center. 2 cups crunchy peanut butter, 1/2 cup margarine, 1 pound confectioners sugar, 3 cups crisp rice cereal. Combine all ingredients except cereal and form into 1-inch balls. Add cereal. Chill and dip in chocolate.

Chocolate Covered Pretzels. Temper white or semi-sweet chocolate and melt to dipping consistency. Drop a few pretzels in and lift out with fork. Hold to let drain slightly. Place on cookie sheet to harden.

Chocolate Covered Nuts. Dip almonds, pecans or other nuts in chocolate. Try tinted, flavored white chocolate.

Threading. Thread a different color chocolate over truffle. Dip fork in melted chocolate. Shake off excess. Drizzle threads of chocolate over dipped candy to make designs. Various threaded designs may be used to identify different truffle centers.

Penoche
Old fashioned candy recipe!

3 cups sugar
1/4 cup corn syrup (light or dark)
3/4 cup milk
2 cups nuts, pecans or peanuts

Caramalize 1 cup sugar by mixing it with 1 tablespoon water and microwaving on HIGH about 2-2 1/2 minutes until it liquifies and is a caramel color. Mix 2 cups sugar with the other ingredients and microwave on HIGH until it boils. Add caramalized sugar and microwave on 70% power 15-20 minutes to soft-ball stage. (Reduce power level to 50% if necessary to keep syrup from boiling over.) Cool slightly and pour into mixer bowl. Beat until candy holds shape. Drop by tablespoonful on a sheet of waxed paper.

Peanut Brittle

Yield: 1 pound

1 cup raw peanuts
1 cup white sugar
1/4 cup white corn syrup
1/4 cup dark corn syrup
1/8 teaspoon salt
1 teaspoon vanilla
1 tablespoon butter
2 teaspoons soda

Stir peanuts, sugar, syrups and salt together in deep bowl. Cook on HIGH 4 minutes. Stir candy so all sugar is mixed and continue cooking on HIGH 3 more minutes. Add butter and vanilla to syrup, blending well. Cook on HIGH 1-3 minutes. Add soda and stir until light and foamy. Pour immediately onto lightly buttered surface, spreading it out. Cool and break into pieces. Store in airtight container. If roasted salted peanuts are used, omit salt and add peanuts after first 4 minutes of cooking.

Pecan Butter Brittle
A must to try! Truly scrumptious!

1 cup sugar
1/2 cup corn syrup
1/4 cup butter
1 inch square paraffin
2 cups pecan halves
2 teaspoons baking soda

Microwave sugar, syrup and butter 3 minutes on HIGH. Stir in paraffin to melt. Stir in nuts. Mix well and microwave on HIGH 7-12 minutes, checking nuts several times to make sure they don't burn. Add soda, quickly stir and pour onto greased surface. Cool and break into pieces. Store in airtight container.

☞ For interesting Brittle variations, try almonds, pecans, peanuts, cashews, walnuts, coconuts or combinations in either of the Brittle recipes. Also try using brown sugar instead of white.

Caramel Popcorn Balls

1 cup light brown sugar
1/4 cup butter
1/2 cup light corn syrup
2/3 cup sweetened condensed milk (1/2 of a 14-ounce can)
1 teaspoon vanilla
4 quarts popped corn

Combine sugar, butter and syrup in a deep bowl. Cook on HIGH 2-3 minutes until butter melts. Add milk and microwave on 70% power until soft ball stage is reached (234°-238°) for 5-7 minutes. Stir in vanilla and pour over popped corn. Mix with buttered hands, roll into balls. Try adding raisins, peanuts or pretzels with the popped corn.

Butterscotch Nut Squares

1 cup (6 ounces) butterscotch chips
1 cup (6 ounce) semi-sweet chocolate chips
1 (14 ounce) can condensed milk
1 cup pecans, chopped
1 teaspoon vanilla
1 cup pecan halves

Combine butterscotch chips, chocolate chips and condensed milk in a 2-quart glass casserole. Microwave on 70% power for 4-6 minutes, stirring occasionally until chips melt and candy begins to thicken. Add chopped nuts and stir to blend. Pour candy into a buttered 8-inch square dish. Top with pecan halves. Chill in refrigerator until firm enough to slice.

Lollipops

10 lollipop sticks
3/4 cup sugar
1/2 cup light corn syrup
1/4 cup butter
1 teaspoon flavoring
    (peppermint, orange, vanilla, cinnamon, etc.)
Food coloring
Cinnamon candies or other miniature candies for decoration

Arrange sticks on parchment paper, spacing at least 4 inches apart. Combine sugar, corn syrup and butter in 2-quart measuring cup or bowl and cook on HIGH 2 minutes. Stir in flavoring and food coloring. Continue cooking on HIGH until candy thermometer registers 270°F. or soft-crack stage, about 5-7 minutes.

Drop syrup by tablespoons over one end of each stick. Press candies gently into place. Let cool completely. Wrap each in plastic. Store in air tight container.

Candied Apples: Use cinnamon flavoring and red coloring. Insert popsicle sticks into about 6 apples and dip the apples one at a time into the cooked candy syrup. Swirl to coat; then stand on waxed paper to cool.

Lollipop molds are fun to use if you have them.

Peanut Butter Squares

1/2 cup graham cracker crumbs
1 cup chunky peanut butter
2 1/2 cups powdered sugar
1 cup melted butter
2 cups milk chocolate chips

Mix crumbs, sugar, butter and peanut butter. Spread in a 9 x 13-inch dish. Shield ends of dish with foil. Microwave on HIGH 2 minutes to set. Melt chocolate by microwaving on 50% power for 3-4 minutes. Spread on above mixture while warm. Chill and cut in squares. If you like Reese's Peanut Butter Cups, you'll love these.

Simply Scrumptious White Fudge

Excellent flavor and versatile. Let it mellow a day or two for full flavor.

Yield: about 60 pieces

1 1/3 cups sugar
1/2 cup butter
2/3 cup cream
1/8 teaspoon salt
1/2 pound white chocolate, finely chopped
2 cups miniature marshmallows
1/2 teaspoon vanilla

Microwave sugar, butter, cream and salt on 50%-70% power about 20-30 minutes or to 238ºF., soft ball stage. Add chocolate, marshmallows and vanilla. Blend well and pack into a 9-inch square pan and cut into squares when partially cool.

Before completely cooled, White Fudge has a pliable texture like dough. It can easily be rolled into balls or other desired shapes for dipping in chocolate.

Make a candy assortment from one recipe using various flavorings and fruits: chopped candied or dried fruits, nuts of any kinds, raisins, dates or coconut.

Maple nut: Add several drops of maple flavoring and finely chopped pecans.

Coffee: Dissolve instant coffee in a few drops of water. Microwave a few seconds if needed.

Divide fudge in half. Flavor and color half as desired. Roll out each half separately. Lay one on top of the other and roll up pinwheel fashion. Chill thoroughly and slice.

Candied Citrus Peel
George Washington's Favorite Candy!
Martha used to make it all the time!

Yield: 2 cups

2 cups peel (orange, grapefruit, lime, etc.)
1 cup sugar
Dash of salt
1/2 cup water

Cut the peel into narrow strips and cover with water. Microwave on HIGH for 10 minutes and drain. Cover with fresh water and microwave on HIGH 10 additional minutes. Add drained peel to 2-quart bowl with sugar and 1/2 cup water. Microwave on HIGH for 12 to 16 minutes, stirring several times. Cool and roll each piece in sugar.

Variation: Add one 3-ounce package of fruit flavored gelatin to sugar and toss citrus in this mixture.

Pecan Pralines

2 cups granulated sugar
1 teaspoon soda
1 cup buttermilk
1/8 teaspoon salt
2 tablespoons butter
2 1/2 cups broken pecans
1 teaspoon vanilla

In deep bowl combine sugar, soda, buttermilk and salt. Microwave on 70% power for about 10 minutes, stirring several times and scraping the sides of the bowl. Add butter and pecans and continue cooking at 70% power about 10-20 minutes, until candy reaches soft-ball stage. Add vanilla. Cool slightly and beat until creamy and slightly thickened. Quickly drop by tablespoonfuls onto waxed paper and let cool.

🌀 High humidity may cause pralines to become sugary.

🌀 Pulverize pralines in blender to make a powder. Store praline powder in a closed jar to have on hand for garnishing cakes, ice cream or other desserts. Praline powder is also good for flavoring cake icings, ice creams and puddings.

Simply Scrumptious
Potpourri

Potpourri
Jams, Jellies & Conserves

Pickles & Relishes

Freezing Fruits & Vegetables

Flowers & Herbs

Children's Treats & Miscellaneous

Jams, Jellies and Relishes

Jams, jellies and relishes cooked in the microwave have a fresh flavor that is not achieved by conventional methods of cooking or processing; therefore you may prefer to microwave small amounts rather than prepare large batches that would require waterbath processing needed for long storage.

Cook in a deep dish. Sterilize jars by filling them half full of water and microwaving on HIGH until the water boils vigorously. Metal jar lids must be treated conventionally following the manufacturers directions.

The doneness test for microwaved jams and jellies is the same "sheet" test as for conventional jams, even when using commercial fruit pectin. Dip a large metal spoon in the boiling jam, holding it up out of the steam and turning the spoon so the syrup runs off the edge. When the drops run together and drop off the spoon in a sheet, the jelling point has been reached.

To seal jelly, pour boiling hot jelly into sterilized hot jars leaving 1/8-inch head space. Screw prepared metal lid on firmly and allow jelly to set upright, undisturbed until cool. A vacuum seal will form as the jelly cools. To minimize the risk of surface mold during long storage time in hot humid climates, process jelly for 5 minutes in a water bath canner (conventional method).

Jellies may be sealed with paraffin. Use only enough paraffin to make a layer 1/8-inch thick. A single, thin layer, which can expand or contract readily, gives a better seal than one thick layer. To seal jelly, pour the hot mixture immediately into a sterilized jar to within 1/2 inch of the top and cover with hot paraffin. Melt paraffin conventionally - not in the microwave.

For jams, conserves or marmalades, remove the product from the microwave and stir gently for 5 minutes. This will allow the syrup to thicken slightly and help keep the fruit dispersed throughout. Skim the foam that appears on the surface. Pour into hot glass containers to within 1/2 inch of top. (This procedure is exactly the same in conventional preserving.) Seal immediately.

For long term storage, jams, preserves, marmalades and conserves should be processed in a boiling water bath (conventional method). Jelly and Jam recipes offered by Simply Scrumptious require 5 minutes processing time.

Simply Scrumptious Strawberry Jam
Wonderful fresh strawberry flavor!

Makes 5 half-pints

1 quart fresh strawberries
3 1/2 cups sugar
4 tablespoons powdered pectin
2 1/2 cups sugar

Wash and stem berries, drain in colander. Crush berries in 2-quart glass bowl. Stir in powdered pectin, sugar and lemon juice. Microwave on HIGH for 8 minutes, stirring several times. Test for doneness using the "sheet" test. Jam is done when it "sheets" from a spoon. Cook longer if needed. Pour into 5 sterilized 1/2-pint jars and seal.

Fresh Peach Jam

Makes 4-5 half-pints

2 cups coarse peach purée (Peel fresh peaches and chop in blender to desired consistency.)
4 tablespoons powdered pectin
2 1/2 cups sugar

Measure 2 cups purée into a 2-quart glass bowl. Stir in pectin. Microwave on HIGH for 2 minutes and 15 seconds. Add sugar and microwave on HIGH 3-4 minutes, stirring several times. Test for "sheet" test. Stir 5 minutes. Pour into sterilized jars and seal.

SPICED PEACH JAM: To "Fresh Peach Jam" add 1/2 teaspoon cinnamon, 1/4 teaspoon cloves, 1/4 teaspoon allspice and 1 tablespoon lemon juice. Good served as a jam on toast, to flavor cream cheese or served with ham or chicken.

Banana Jam
Great with peanut butter sandwiches or ice cream!

Makes 1 pint

3 cups sliced, ripe bananas
1 1/2 cups sugar
1/4 cup orange juice
3 tablespoons lemon juice
1 small cinnamon stick
2 whole cloves

Combine all ingredients in a deep bowl. Microwave on HIGH until sugar dissolves, 5-10 minutes, stirring several times. Continue cooking on HIGH until thickened, about 8-12 minutes. Pour into jars and let stand until set. Refrigerate.

Berry Jam

Blueberry, blackberry, boysenberry, raspberry, gooseberry, loganberry.

Makes 4 cups

3 cups fresh berries, washed and drained
1 tablespoon lemon juice
1/2 (1 3/4 ounce) package powdered pectin
2 1/2 cups sugar

Wash berries in a deep bowl. Stir in lemon juice and pectin. Microwave on HIGH 10-15 minutes, stirring several times or until mixture comes to a full, rolling boil. Stir in sugar. Microwave on HIGH 5-7 minutes or until mixture returns to a full boil and reaches "sheet" test. Pour into sterilized jars and seal.

For seedless jam, crushed berries may be microwaved until soft and pressed through a sieve or food grinder; then add lemon juice and pectin and proceed as above.

Pineapple Jam

Makes about 5 cups

1 (20-ounce) can unsweetened, crushed pineapple or
3 cups finely chopped fresh pineapple
   (about 1 large pineapple)
3 1/4 cups sugar
1/2 lemon, thinly sliced
3 ounces liquid fruit pectin
1 cup chopped walnuts (optional)

Combine ingredients except nuts and microwave on HIGH for 12-15 minutes or until pineapple is no longer crisp. Add walnuts and stir until thickened. Pour into sterilized jars, and seal with paraffin.

Mango Jam

1 1/2 cups mango purée (Fruit peeled and chopped in blender to desired
   consistency.)
1 1/3 cups sugar
3 tablespoons powdered pectin

Combine 1/2 cup purée with pectin in a 2-quart bowl. Microwave on HIGH about 1 1/2 minutes or to hard boil. Stir in sugar and remaining purée; cook 3 minutes, stirring several times. Microwave on HIGH to a hard boil. Stir 5 minutes and pour into sterilized jars and seal.

CHESTNUTS: Slash crosswise through skin on flat end of chestnut shell. In a glass pie plate, arrange 20-25 chestnuts on plate. Microwave on HIGH 3-4 minutes, stirring every minute until nuts are soft when squeezed. Rest 5 minutes. Peel and eat warm.

Bouquet Garni Jelly

Makes 3-4 cups

3 1/4 cups sugar
1 cup water
1/2 cup red wine vinegar
2 Bouquet Garni (See page 205.)
3 ounces liquid fruit pectin

Combine sugar, water, vinegar and Bouquet Garni and microwave on HIGH about 5-7 minutes or until mixture boils. Stir in pectin. Bring back to a boil and continue cooking until jelly "sheets" off a spoon, about 5-10 minutes. Pour into sterilized jars and seal. Serve with meat. Good on a cold meat tray.

Cinnamon Jelly

Makes 4-5 cups

2 cups apple juice
2 1/2 cups sugar
1 (1 3/4-ounce) package fruit pectin
2 tablespoons lemon juice
1 cup red cinnamon candies or
    1/2 cup Red Hots

Combine apple juice, sugar and fruit pectin in a deep bowl. Microwave on HIGH 5-7 minutes or until mixture boils. Add remaining ingredients and stir until candy dissolves. Microwave on HIGH 5-10 minutes or to "sheet" test. Skim and pour into sterilized jars and seal. Reduce power level during cooking if needed to prevent boiling over.

APPLE JELLY: Prepare Cinnamon Jelly omitting the cinnamon candies or Red Hots, and reduce pectin to 1/2 package.

Green Pepper Jelly

Yield 4 cups

2 medium bell peppers
3/4 cup cider vinegar
3 1/4 cups sugar
2 tablespoons fresh hot pepper or
    1-2 tablespoons crushed dried pepper
3 ounces liquid fruit pectin
Green food coloring

Remove seeds from pepper. Grind peppers in blender. Mix with vinegar, sugar and hot pepper. Microwave on HIGH 5-10 minutes or to rolling boil. Add liquid pectin and continue microwaving on HIGH until mixture comes to a full rolling boil again; cook for 1 minute.

Pour through strainer into bowl, spoon off foam and add a few drops of green food coloring. Pour into sterilized jars and seal. Serve on top of cream cheese with crackers or with meats and vegetables.

Wear gloves when handling hot peppers.

Peach Honey
Delicious served with meat dishes!

Makes about 1 pint

2 cups chopped ripe peaches
2 cups sugar
1 tablespoon lemon juice

Combine peaches and sugar in deep bowl. Microwave on HIGH until sugar dissolves, 5-10 minutes, stirring several times. Add lemon juice and continue cooking on HIGH until thickened, about 6-12 minutes. Stir several times. Pour into jars and let stand until set. Refrigerate. Serve just as you would cranberry sauce.

Plum Conserve

Makes 2 1/2 cups

1 pound plums, pitted and chopped
1 orange, seeded and chopped
2 tablespoons thinly sliced orange peel (optional)
1/2 cup sugar or to taste
1/2 cup chopped walnuts or pecans (optional)

Microwave plums, sugar, oranges and orange rind, covered tightly with plastic wrap on HIGH 8 minutes, stirring once. Stir in nuts, re-cover and microwave on HIGH 2 minutes longer or until peel is transparent. Let stand covered 5 minutes. Chill.

Cranberry-Orange Relish

Yield 8-10 servings

1 pound fresh cranberries
2 medium oranges
2 cups sugar
1 cup chopped nuts (optional)

Quarter oranges, remove seeds and chop in blender. Clean cranberries. Place all ingredients In a deep dish and microwave on HIGH 15-20 minutes or until cranberries are soft. Stir several times. Store in refrigerator.

Banana Pops
Delicious and nutritious snack.

Cut banana in half crosswise. Push popsicle stick in each and freeze. When ready to serve, place in microwave for about 10-15 seconds to soften the peel. Don't overcook or banana will become soft. Peel with a knife. Serve plain or you may dip the banana in melted chocolate to serve; or dip in chocolate and roll in chopped nuts or granola.

Pint O' Pickles

Makes 1 pint

1/2 cup cider vinegar
1/4 cup sugar
1/2 teaspoon salt
1 teaspoon mixed pickling spice
2 1/2 cups sliced cucumbers
1 small onion, thinly sliced

Microwave vinegar, sugar and spices on HIGH 4 minutes, stirring once. Add cucumbers and onion. Stir to coat. Cover with plastic wrap and microwave on HIGH 3 minutes. Stir, re-cover, and cook on HIGH 1 minute longer. Let stand, covered for 10 minutes. Spoon into jar, cover and chill before serving.

Fresh Corn Relish

Makes 1 cup

1 1/3 cups fresh-cut corn
1/2 cup finely diced celery
1 tablespoon chopped green pepper
4 tablespoons vinegar
2 tablespoons sugar
1/2 teaspoon salt
1/8 teaspoon pepper
5 tablespoons chopped onion
1/8 teaspoon tumeric
2 tablespoons chopped canned pimento

Cook corn by microwaving covered on HIGH 2-5 minutes. Add all remaining ingredients except pimento and microwave on HIGH to heat thoroughly. It is not necessary to boil mixture. Add pimento. Cool and refrigerate. This makes a colorful side dish to be eaten with vegetables or served as a salad. It improves with age!

Onion Pepper Relish

Makes about 2 cups

1 small sweet red pepper
1 small sweet green pepper
2 onions, chopped
1/2 cup vinegar
1/4 cup sugar
1/2 teaspoon salt
1/4 teaspoon crushed red pepper
1 bay leaf

Wash, seed and dice peppers. Stir all ingredients together in a deep bowl. Cover and microwave on HIGH for 5 minutes. Stir, reduce power to 70% and cook covered for 10 minutes longer. Let stand, covered 5 minutes. Remove bay leaf, stir and store in the refrigerator.

Jiffy Spiced Fruit
Good fresh flavor!

3 large peaches, pears, apricots or nectarines, peeled and halved
1/2 cup cider vinegar
1/3 cup sugar
1/4 teaspoon ginger
1 (3-inch) cinnamon stick
6 whole cloves

Combine vinegar, sugar, and spices in a deep bowl. Cover with plastic wrap and microwave on HIGH for 4 minutes or until sugar dissolves, stirring several times. Add fruit and stir to coat with syrup. Re-cover and cook on HIGH 6 minutes or until fruit is tender. Cool and refrigerate overnight to blend flavors. Serve chilled as a meat accompaniment or on the relish tray. Will keep in the refrigerator up to a month. Remove spices after second week.

అ౧౦౧అ౧౦౧౦అ౧అ౧ అ

S'mores

2 graham cracker squares
Chocolate chips or other milk chocolate candy
1 large marshmallow

Place 1 graham cracker square on a paper napkin. Top with chocolate and marshmallow. Microwave on HIGH - just until marshmallow puffs up, about 20 seconds. Top with second cracker. Peanut butter or sliced bananas may also be added, if desired.

Homemade Condensed Milk
Make your own to save $$$ or avoid a trip to the store.

1/2 cup cold water
1 1/3 cups dry milk
3/4 cup sugar
1 teaspoon vanilla

Stir water and dry milk together. Microwave on HIGH 1 minute. Stir in sugar and vanilla and cook on HIGH 1 - 2 1/2 minutes to dissolve sugar and thicken. Cool to use. Store covered in refrigerator up to 1 week. Yield is equal to 1 (14-ounce) can sweetened condensed milk.

Warm baby food in seconds. Remove lid from jar, microwave on HIGH 25-40 seconds. Dense foods, such as liver, may need to be removed from the jar and covered with waxed paper to reduce popping.

If nail polish cap is stuck, microwave on HIGH 5-10 seconds.

Freezing Fruits and Vegetables

The microwave oven is a good partner with the home garden. It is a real convenience when preparing small amounts of food for the freezer. You may prefer to use the traditional boiling water method when freezing large quantities. However, remember that only 2-3 pints of vegetables should be blanched at one time, even conventionally.

Vegetables require scalding (blanching) to stop the action of natural enzymes that cause changes in the food. Blanching prolongs the storage life of the food. Vegetables may be blanched in the microwave without the large amounts of boiling water required conventionally; therefore, they retain water soluble vitamins, flavor and texture that is lost in conventional methods. Follow suggested blanching times. Both over-blanching and under-blanching reduce quality.

General Procedure: Prepare vegetables, wash, peel, slice or cube. Blanch only one pound or one quart at a time. Place vegetables and water in a dish and cover. Do not add salt. Microwave the suggested time, stirring halfway through blanching. Place vegetables in ice-cold water to cool them quickly and immediately stop the cooking process. Let them stay in the cold water a few minutes, or until cooled. Drain thoroughly. Package, label, and quick freeze. Be sure to use a moisture-vapor proof packaging material.

BLANCHING CHART

Vegetable	Quantity	Amount Water	Minutes on HIGH
Asparagus	1 pound	1/4 cup	2 1/2 - 4
Beans	1 pound (3 cups)	1/2 cup	3 1/2 - 5 1/2
Broccoli	1 pound (1 bunch)	1/2 cup	3 - 5
Carrots, sliced	1 pound (6-8)	1/4 cup	3 1/2 - 5 1/2
Cauliflower (flowerets)	1 pound (1 head)	none	3 - 5
Corn-on-the-cob	4 ears	none	3 1/2 - 4 1/2
Corn, whole kernel or cream style	4 ears, cut off		3 1/2-5
		1/4 cup	
Peas, green	2 cups	none	3 1/2 - 5
Spinach	1 pound	1/4 cup	2 - 3 1/2
Squash	1 pound		3 - 4 1/2

For vegetables not specifically mentioned, allow 3-4 minutes per pound.

Pre-cook or blanch cream style corn in the microwave to avoid scorching and the need for continuous stirring.

When cooking foods frozen in a cooking pouch, it is not necessary to drop them in boiling water. Just puncture the top of the bag to make a steam vent, place the pouch on a plate to catch drips and microwave on HIGH the amount of time needed.

When canning foods that require conventional hot water bath or pressure canner methods of processing, heat the food in the microwave oven and hot pack the jars - instead of cold packing to reduce the processing time and avoid excess heat in the kitchen. (Always process canned food by conventional methods. Processing jars of food in the microwave is not recommended.)

Sweet Woodruff Potpourri

1 cup sweet woodruff
1/2 cup lemon verbena
1/2 cup geranium
1/8 cup orris root
1/4 cup mint
2 drops lemon verbena oil

Combine dried leaves in a bowl. Place orris root on top, add drops of oil, mix thoroughly. Store in tightly sealed jar in a dark place for 4-6 weeks, shaking jar every other day.

Potpourri Wreath

Gives off a subtle fragrance for many months. A delightful and unique way to display your "microwave dried" flowers in any room of your house.

Materials needed:

Straw wreath base
Florist pins (U-shaped)
Spanish moss (optional)
Fresh herbs of your choice:
    rosemary, sage, tansy, many
    varieties of thyme, fennel,
    lavender, etc. (Do not use rue!
    It has an overwhelming fragrance.)
Dried flowers on wire stems
Other dried "filler" materials:
    baby's breath, eucalyptus, citrus
    spirals, clove-studded sweetgum
    balls, whole nutmeg on wire stems, etc.

Directions:

Take the green plastic wrapping off the straw wreath base. Mash or push the wreath into the desired shape. (We have made triangular and oval wreaths.) Attach a small block of styrofoam with pins at the base. This will provide a place to attach a "bouquet of flowers." Wrap a wire around the top of the wreath to form a hanger.

Using florist pins, cover the wreath with Spanish moss. This step is not necessary if moss is unavailable, but it covers the straw and enables you to use less fresh herb sprigs.

Using florist pins, attach sprigs of fresh herbs to cover the wreath. Overlap the herbs so the pins do not show. They will dry naturally on the wreath.

Attach flowers and filler materials to form a floral spray. Spritz lightly with clear acrylic spray to protect the flowers from humidity and to preserve the colors.

Preserving Flowers and Foliage

The microwave oven enables you to dry flowers in a matter of minutes—which would take weeks conventionally! The quality is superior, the colors are brighter and the flowers are not as dry and perishable as conventionally dried ones.

Selecting flowers: Flowers that dry especially well are roses, zinnias, asters, pansies, daisies, violets, carnations, daffodils, marigolds and chrysanthemums. Some flowers difficult to dry are tulips, irises and geraniums. Select flowers with bright colors; pick them just as they are reaching their peak of bloom. Avoid flowers with thick or densely clustered centers.

Drying agents:

Silica-Gel, available in many hobby shops, is the most satisfactory material. This is what we recommend using for the best quality dried flowers.

Borax/Cornmeal mixture, containing equal amounts of each can be used if Silica-Gel is not available.

Sifted Kitty Litter, made of ground clay, has a great deal of absorbing quality and can be used.

Each of these may be reused over and over.

Procedure:

Dry 3-4 flowers at a time. Select a microwave-safe container deep enough so the drying agent can cover the entire blooms. Pour the drying agent into a container to 1/2 inch deep. Cut each flower stem to 1/2 inch length. Place the flowers, head up, in the drying agent. With a spoon, gently sprinkle the agent around the outside of each flower until the bottom half is covered all around. Sprinkle the agent inside each flower and between the petals. Use a toothpick to separate the petals if needed. Place a cup of water in the corner of the oven to provide moisture in the oven. Place the flowers, completely covered with drying agent, in the oven, uncovered, and microwave about 1-3 minutes.

Many variables affect drying time, such as the amount of moisture in the flowers and the size of the flowers. You can determine the appropriate drying time only through experimentation.

Standing time is necessary for the flowers to cool off and set. After heating, let the flowers stand, undisturbed, in the drying agent for 1-2 hours to overnight. Some flowers give better results with a longer standing time. When the flowers are "set", gently spoon away the drying agent to expose the flowers. Gently remove the flowers and lightly brush the flower petals with a soft artist brush to remove particles of the drying agent.

A spray coloring agent or powdered tempra may be applied to add more color, if desired, but this is usually not needed since the colors of microwave-dried flowers are usually vivid. A coloring may be used months or years later to "freshen" the arrangement, since the colors do tend to fade with time.

When flowers are dry, attach floral wires for stems. Make a hook in one end of the wire and pull it through the center of the flower with the hook-end embedded in the center. Use floral tape to secure the flower to the wire. A "glue gun" is very handy for this if one is available. Just hold the stem wire against the flower stem and touch with the glue gun, instantly gluing the two together. Then use florist tape.

Drying without a drying agent: Fall leaves can be dried in the microwave without a drying agent, since they already have a low moisture content. Just place paper towels in the bottom of your oven, then layer leaves with paper towels to make several layers. Use as large a spray of leaves as will easily fit in the oven. Microwave on HIGH 1 - 1 1/2 minutes. If needed, turn the leaves and paper towels over and microwave 1 - 1 1/2 minutes longer. Check the leaves to prevent over-drying. Magnolia branches and leaves, ferns and camelia foliage may be dried by this method also. Do not use recycled paper towels.

Herbs: Wash herb leaves to be dried and drain well. Place a few sprigs or a half-cup between two paper towels and microwave on HIGH about 2 minutes or until dry.

Bouquet Garni

Makes 1

2 cloves garlic, halved
1 bay leaf
4 sprigs parsley
2 teaspoons snipped fresh thyme or
3/4 teaspoon dried thyme

Cut a small square from several thicknesses of cheesecloth and place the ingredients in the center. Bring corners of cheesecloth together to form a bag. Tie with string.

Williamsburg Potpourri

Potpourri is a mixture of dried flowers and leaves seasoned with spices and oils. They are kept in a covered jar to fill the room with fragrance when the lid is lifted.

1 quart flower petals
1 ounce each: cinnamon, nutmeg,
cloves and ginger-root
1/2 ounce anise seed
2 ounces powdered arrowroot
Whole cloves
Crushed cinnamon sticks

Spice Wreath
Adds an elegant Williamsburg touch in your home.

Materials needed:

Wreath base: straw, styrofoam, wood or 4 or 5 circles of corrugated cardboard, glued together. Straw and styrofoam bases give depth to the wreath and look better.

Linoleum Paste: (That's right - paste used for gluing down linoleum!)

A collection of nuts, cones (whole and rosettes), interesting seed pods, dried flowers, spices and herbs. Use your imagaination to think of interesting dry materials to use. Here are a few suggestions:

1. Use acorn caps as little cups to hold spices such as coriander, dill seed, fennel, mustard seed, etc.

2. Citrus spirals: Cut a long narrow strip from a lemon, lime, grapefruit or orange peel. Wrap strip tightly around a wooden skewer. Microwave 5-6 spirals for 1-3 minutes until dried. Slip them off the skewer and they will retain a corkscrew shape. These are attractive in wreaths and in dried arrangements.

3. Dried flowers (Rose buds and baby's breath are nice. Your choice!)

4. Clove-studded sweetgum balls: Dip whole cloves in white glue and push into sweetgum balls. (These are good in Holiday arrangements too.)

5. Potpourri puffs: Wrap about a tablespoon of herbs in a 5-inch square of net and tie with a narrow ribbon.

6. Spices: Whole nutmeg, cinnamon sticks, star anise, 4 or 5 pods of cardamon glued on a wire, etc.

Directions:
Attach a hanger to the wreath base. Using an old paint brush or disposable spoon, spread the linoleum paste generously over the top and sides of the wreath base. Let it dry 15-20 minutes; then stick on dried materials and spices. It takes several days for the linoleum paste to hard-dry. You may go back as it dries and, using white glue, add additional spices and other materials to fill in.

 This is an excellent time to inventory your spice rack and use old spices.

Jennifer's Jingerbread House

1 (14.5 ounce) box gingerbread mix
1 cup all-purpose flour
1 tablespoon ginger
1 tablespoon cinnamon
1 teaspoon lemon flavoring
2/3 cup water

Stir dry ingredients together. Add water and thoroughly mix. Chill dough 2 hours. Roll out to 1/8-inch thickness on a piece of lightly floured waxed paper. Cut out the shapes and remove the excess dough. Tear the waxed paper between the gingerbread pieces so that you can cook one piece at a time. Cut out desired doors and windows. Microwave each piece on 50% power for 4-6 minutes, depending on the size of the piece. Cool completely before assembling.

Icing:

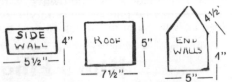

4 egg whites
5 cups sifted powdered sugar
1/2 teaspoon cream of tartar

Beat egg whites until stiff, slowly sifting in powdered sugar and cream of tartar while beating. Keep covered with a damp towel when not using so it won't dry out. To assemble, "glue" one end and one side together with icing. Prop it up and allow about 30 minutes to dry. Repeat with the other end and side. Attach the four walls together and add the roof, allowing sufficient drying time between each addition. Decorate as desired, using candies and cookies, pretzels for logs, icing-covered cones for trees, etc.

If the Jingerbread House is not to be eaten, a glue gun makes assembly quick and easy.

Martin's Play Dough

2 cups flour, sifted
2 cups water
1 cup salt
4 teaspoons cream of tartar
2 tablespoons oil
Food coloring

Mix all ingredients and microwave 3-5 minutes on HIGH, stirring every minute, until it is so thick you can no longer stir it. Knead and store in airtight container. It keeps for months.

Paste

1/2 cup flour
1 cup water
1/2 teaspoon mint flavoring

Mix and microwave on HIGH about 2 minutes. Stir several times. It will appear to thicken all at once. If a thinner consistency is desired, thin down with cold water.

Baked Dough Ornaments

4 cups all-purpose flour
1 cup salt
1 1/2 cups water
Food coloring (optional) or
Instant tea for a toasted color (optional)
1 teaspoon powdered alum

Combine all ingredients. Knead about 5 minutes until smooth. Roll out dough to about 1/4 inch thickness on waxed paper. Cut out 7-9 designs. Remove excess dough. Microwave on 50% power for 4-6 minutes. The size of the ornaments will determine the cooking time. Turn the ornaments over to dry the under side. Microwave a few minutes longer if needed. Ornaments may be painted with acrylic paints and sprayed with clear high-gloss acryllic paint or varnish to seal out moisture.

Kim's Finger Paint

3 tablespoons sugar
1/2 cup cornstarch
2 cups cold water
Powdered tempera or food coloring*

Mix sugar and cornstarch, stirring in water. Cook on HIGH about 4 minutes, stirring several times. Mixture will appear to thicken instantly. Add coloring and a pinch of detergent to facilitate clean-up.

*We prefer tempera because it stains less than food coloring; however, either may be used.

Finger Paint

1/2 cup dry laundry starch
1/4 cup cold water
1 1/2 cups boiling water (microwave 3-4 minutes)
1/2 cup soapflakes
1 teaspoon glycerine
Food coloring or powdered tempera (we prefer tempera)

Mix starch and cold water. Pour in boiling water and microwave on HIGH about 3-6 minutes or until shiny. Add soap and glycerine. Add coloring.

Darrick's Modeling Clay

1 cup cornstarch
2 cups baking soda (1 pound)
1 1/4 cups cold water
Food coloring (optional)

Stir together and microwave on HIGH 4-6 minutes or until mixture thickens to mashed potato consistency. Remove from heat and turn out on a board and cover with a damp cloth until cool. Knead like bread dough. Keep in air-tight container. Clay becomes hard when left out. Children can form objects, leave out overnight and paint the next day with tempera or acrylics. Paint with varnish or clear nail polish to seal.

Modeling Goop

2 cups salt
2/3 cup water
1 cup cornstarch
1/2 cup cold water

Combine salt and 2/3 cup water. Microwave on HIGH about 1-3 minutes or until salt is dissolved. Add cornstarch and 1/2 cup water. Stir until smooth. Cook on HIGH until thick. Store in plastic bag. Will not crumble when dry.

Cornstarch Modeling Clay

1 cup salt
1/2 cup cornstarch
1/2 cup boiling water (add food coloring to water if desired)

Mix cornstarch and salt. Stir in water. Microwave on HIGH, stirring several times, until mixture is too stiff to stir. When cooled, knead until smooth. Store in air-tight container and refrigerate.

Herb Sachet

Mix equal amounts of rosemary, thyme and mint. Add some ground cloves. Tie in a little sachet bag.

To soften old dried-up shoe polish, remove from metal container and microwave on HIGH 10-15 seconds.

Soften soap tidbits in a little water in microwave on HIGH 1-2 minutes to utilize leftovers. Mold into bar or ball when soft.

Squeeze-easy fruit: Fruits such as oranges, lemons and limes are easier to squeeze if they are at room temperature or slightly warm. Microwave one on HIGH for 30 seconds.

Index

Index 211

Index 213

Notes

Notes

Notes

Notes

Notes

Notes

Notes

Notes

Notes

About the Authors

Mary Ann Feuchter Robinson, Rosemary Dunn Stancil, and Lorela
Nichols Wilkins all hold college degrees in home economics. Together,
they have more than twenty years of experience in conducting cooking
and microwave cooking classes for gourmet shops, leading department
stores, garden clubs, women's organizations, adult education groups
and television shows throughout the country.